Mad Dogs & Englishmen

A year of things to see and do in England

Mad Dogs & Englishmen

A year of things to see and do in England

TOM JONES

10 9 8 7 6 5 4 3

First published in the UK in 2013 by Virgin Books, an imprint of Ebury Publishing
A Random House Group Company

Addresses for companies within The Random House Group Limited can be found
at www.randomhouse.co.uk

The Random House Group Limited Reg. No. 954009

A CIP catalogue record for this book is available from the British Library

ISBN: 9780753541746

Design: Lottie Crumbleholme
Illustrations © Hannah Warren, 2013
Photography © Tom Jones, 2013

Printed and bound in Italy by Printer Trento

To buy books by your favourite authors and register for offers, visit
www.randomhouse.co.uk

Please note: Where text refers to 'Nearest station', this is the nearest mainline
station, not local rail, which in some instances may be nearer to the destination.

CONTENTS

For Sue & Pete

ACKNOWLEDGEMENTS

With thanks to Hannah Knowles, Nicola Barr, Lottie Crumbleholme, Hannah Warren and Virgin Books for their help in making this book. Thanks as always to Susan, Peter & Cynthia Jones for their help and support, and for, along with the late Ronald Jones, teaching me to love interesting places.

Thanks to Stephen Jones, Jemima Warren, Ronald Whittington, Jon Searle and Alison Gregory for joining me in different corners of England, Paul Warbrick for offering me shelter in Manchester and the Lakes and Lis Wood for entertaining me in Bristol. Thanks also to Rosie Luff for her knowledge of Worcestershire and the staff and guests at Gladstone's Library for their hospitality.

INTRODUCTION

Many think they know England, but few have travelled it fully, often overlooking the depth of culture, geology, geography and history in the country on their doorstep. However, England still has the potential to amaze and delight even the most cynical traveller with displays of the unexpected, from the real snow ski slopes of Cumbria to the sub-tropical gardens of the Isles of Scilly.

Whilst it can be driven end to end in half a day, England offers almost unlimited landscapes, a rich cultural heritage, and a diversity of opportunities any nation would struggle to match.

England inspires with its constantly changing scenery, which has touched the greatest artists in history; visitors to galleries in even the most remote corners of the country are greeted with outstanding examples of art and architecture.

England's landscapes have also informed the world's finest literature and poetry, with writers capturing their evocative surroundings, from the Kent of Dickens to the Yorkshire of the Brontës and the Cumbria of Wordsworth.

Our deceptively small nation requires more than a second look. This book is an attempt to investigate what can easily be missed or overlooked – forgotten England, if you like. Ours is a country that embraces the changing seasons and reveals its best side, whatever the weather.

This book is the result of thirty years of exploring England and many months of revisiting it to check it was all still there. I hope in some small way these pages encourage you to find an England of your own.

Tom Jones – January 2013

January

With the feasts of December petering out towards Twelfth Night, January brings in the year with vigour: wassailing ceremonies offer a toast to the coming year's crop in England's orchards, while Plough Monday marks the traditional return to work for the year. A month of rich wintry sunsets, January's grey skies are occasionally punctured by blissful days of heavenly blue.

This is a month of crystal clarity, sometimes marked by beautiful frozen spells of snow and ice. The countryside, however, offers an unexpectedly warm welcome to visitors willing to wrap up, and far from the deep-winter slumber of towns and villages they will find misty mornings, muddy puddles, windblown cheeks and rich hospitality beside roaring pub fires.

Watch the Mappleton Bridge Jump

Each New Year's Day, the Derbyshire village of Mappleton (sometimes spelled Mapleton), near Ashbourne, is the venue for an unusual race. Pairs of participants paddle half a mile down the River Dove in small boats before jumping thirty feet from the bridge into the icy cold water.

Following the jump, competitors race across a field to the Okeover Arms to warm up, with the winner receiving the Brass Monkey Trophy. The race was devised by local man Jim Breeze in the 1980s and is now a popular local event, with many of those taking part adopting fancy dress.

Website: www.visitashbourne.co.uk
Address: The Okeover Arms, Mappleton, Ashbourne DE6 2AB
Nearest station: Derby

Drink at the Black Bull, Frosterley

At the Black Bull pub in Frosterley, County Durham, the clocks could have stopped in the nineteenth century: its ageless interior features cosy open fires burning in iron ranges, traditional rooms, flagstone floors and warming ales, making it an atmospheric place for a snug winter's evening.

The Black Bull is only a short walk from the historic Weardale railway, and, as well as attracting steam enthusiasts, the pub is also popular with bell-ringers due to its unique peal of traditional bells housed in the roof, rung by rope and wheel, and not found in any other pub in the world.

Website: www.blackbullfrosterley.com
Address: The Black Bull Inn, Frosterley, Co.Durham, DL13 2SL
Nearest station: Darlington

ATTEND THE BOLNEY WASSAIL

The old English tradition of wassailing sees cider-apple trees blessed for the new season by those hoping to ensure a strong crop, and in the Sussex village of Bolney it is still celebrated with a vocal display on the first Saturday in January.

Known locally as 'Apple Howling', the ancient custom was believed to drive out evil spirits who might compromise the apple crop. Essential to the tradition is consumption of cider and cake, and a torchlight procession featuring the last carols of the season.

Website: www.crmm.org.uk
Address: Old Mill Fruit Farm, Cowfold Road, Bolney, West Sussex RH17 5SE
Nearest station: Haywards Heath

Watch the Pantomime at the City Varieties Music Hall

The Grade II*-listed City Varieties Music Hall in Leeds is the longest continuously operating music hall in Britain, having been opened above the White Swan Inn off Briggate by Charles Thornton in 1865. Originally known as the New Music Hall and Fashionable Lounge, the music hall became City Varieties in 1893.

Probably best known as the venue for BBC television show *The Good Old Days* between 1953 and 1983, the stage has witnessed performances by everyone from Charlie Chaplin to Harry Houdini, Mickey Rooney, Ken Dodd and Barry Cryer, and its annual pantomime season is especially popular with local crowds.

Website: www.cityvarieties.co.uk
Address: City Varieties Music Hall, Swan St, Leeds LS1 6LW
Nearest station: Leeds

Go Skiing at Yad Moss

England is hardly known for its skiing climate, but adventurous skiers have been enjoying the slopes at Yad Moss, near Alston in Cumbria, since the 1970s. England's largest ski area is staffed entirely by volunteers and consists of eight runs, each around half a mile in length.

Despite being in the North Pennines, the slopes can offer some great skiing when the conditions are right, and those expecting an amateur experience should think again, as a Lottery grant has funded the purchase of a 'piste basher' to prepare the slopes, while a permanent button lift is on hand to tow skiers to the top.

Website: www.yadmoss.co.uk
Address: On the B6277, 7 miles south of Alston
Nearest station: Darlington

Watch the Goathland Plough Stots

One of the oldest traditional Yorkshire longsword dance teams in the country, the Goathland Plough Stots hold their annual Day of Dance in the North Yorkshire village of Goathland in mid-January.

This festive occasion, with live musicians and seasonal drinks and food, makes January a busy time for the Stots, who owe their name to the ancient practice of dancers performing on Plough Monday, the Monday after 6 January.

Website: www.goathlandploughstots.co.uk
Address: Goathland Village
Nearest station: Whitby

Climb Big Ben

Built in the 1830s as the crowning glory of Charles Barry's Neo-Gothic Palace of Westminster, the tower – known colloquially as Big Ben and officially renamed Elizabeth Tower in 2012 in honour of the Queen's Jubilee – stands nearly 100 metres tall in the centre of London and has four identical faces.

Tours run regularly and can be arranged through your Member of Parliament, allowing visitors to climb 334 stone steps to hear the real Big Ben – the bell inside the tower – strike the hour.

Website: www.parliament.uk/bigben
Address: Westminster Palace, Parliament Square, London SW1A 0AA
Nearest underground station: Westminster

Listen for the Lost Bells of Dunwich

Once a major port on the Suffolk coast, Dunwich was hit by a fierce storm in early January 1286, sweeping much of the town into the sea. Further storms in 1287 and 1328 destroyed the port, eventually leaving only a few houses and the ruined priory, which remain standing to this day.

Local legend has it that, from Dunwich's bleak stretch of beach, the bells of the submerged church can be heard ringing underwater, forewarning of future storms, while shadowy figures seen on the cliff tops are thought to be the ghosts of former townspeople.

Website: www.dunwich.org.uk
Address: Dunwich, Suffolk
Nearest station: Darsham

SEE THE STRAW BEARS OF WHITTLESEA

The annual Straw Bear Festival is a highlight in the Cambridgeshire town of Whittlesea, during which mysterious figures stalk the streets dressed from head to toe in straw. The festival derives from an annual custom to mark Plough Tuesday, the day after Plough Monday, when farmers traditionally began to plough their fields for the new season, and a straw-covered man (the Bear) was led from house to house to dance for money, food and beer.

Though the resurrected custom takes place on the closest weekend to Plough Tuesday rather than on the day itself, it still maintains the atmosphere of the original, with the Bear wandering the streets and dancing with Morris Men, and much ale and folk music taken in local pubs over the weekend.

Website: www.strawbear.org.uk
Address: Whittlesea Straw Bear Festival Tickets, 4 Delph Street, Whittlesey, Peterborough, PE7 1QQ
Nearest station: Whittlesea

Notes

Seek Sanctuary in Durham

Mounted on the north door of Durham Cathedral, the Sanctuary Knocker is a ferocious metal beast, once the last point of refuge for the accused. Established as early as the ninth century by King Guthred, the right of sanctuary meant that an alleged criminal who reached the cathedral and grasped the ring held in the ornamental knocker's mouth could receive 37 days' sanctuary.

The accused would then have the right to stay within the boundaries of the cathedral for that time – as well as being given food, drink and bedding – and records show that more than 300 criminals sought this protection between 1464 and 1524. This option is not open to modern-day criminals, however, as the right was abolished in 1623.

Website: www.durhamcathedral.co.uk
Address:Durham Cathedral, Palace Green, Durham DH1 3EP
Nearest station: Durham

Visit Lindisfarne Priory

The days around the Feast of St Ceolwulf of Northumbria on 15 January are an atmospheric time to visit Lindisfarne Priory, the final resting place of St Ceowulf, the eighth-century King of Northumbria. The historic monastery was founded on Holy Island by St Aidan in AD 635 as an early outpost of Christianity in Northern England, which was at the time subject to frequent Viking raids.

A deeply pious man, known for his long beard, Ceolwulf reigned for just eight years before abdicating to enter the monastery, and remained there for twenty years until his death, happily undertaking religious study to the sounds of the winds and waves of the North Sea.

Website: www.lindisfarne.org.uk
Address: Holy Island, Berwick-Upon-Tweed, Northumberland TD15 2RX
Nearest station: Berwick-Upon-Tweed

Watch Ships from Spurn Point

As visitors arrive at Spurn Point, the remote end of a three-mile sand-and-shingle spit, and see the peaceful mouth of the Humber before them, it is hard to imagine the spot being a hive of activity, but for hundreds of years passing ships have relied on the point to ensure their safety, as demonstrated by the presence of the Humber RNLI base and the now-disused Spurn Lighthouse.

As well as tracing the routes of the stalking hulks approaching Hull's container ports, the bleak spit also offers the chance to watch wildlife at the Spurn Observatory and to trace the point's First World War coastal artillery batteries, which once protected the Humber in a very different way.

Website: www.spurnpoint.com
Address: Spurn Point, Spurn, near Kilnsea, Humberside HU12 0UB
Nearest station: Hull

Stay at Hartington Hall

A seventeenth-century manor house in the heart of the Derbyshire Peak District, Hartington Hall was built for the Bateman family, who were major landowners. The style of the hall is everything one would expect from an aristocratic country house, with the only significant change to the exterior being the rebuilding of the west front in the nineteenth century.

The Bateman family remained at the house until the early twentieth century, but, in 1934, the building became one of the Youth Hostels Association's first premises. Today, still characterised by log fires and oak panelling, Hartington Hall is one of the finest in the YHA's care, offering quality budget accommodation.

Website: www.yha.org.uk/hostel/hartington
Address: Hall Bank, Hartington, Buxton, Derbyshire, SK17 0AT
Nearest station: Buxton

Go Stargazing at Kielder Observatory

Kielder Forest in Northumberland has the darkest night skies in England, and the Kielder Observatory on Black Fell near the Scottish border was opened in 2008 to take advantage of the lack of light pollution.

Operated by Kielder Observatory Astronomical Society, the observatory holds regular stargazing events, using its various turrets and telescopes to achieve the best possible views of the night sky.

Website: www.kielderobservatory.org
Address: Kielder Observatory, Kielder Forest, Northumberland NE48 1ER
Nearest station: Hexham

VISIT THE PUB WITH NO BEER

A last remaining vestige of the Victorian temperance movement can be found in the Lancashire town of Rawtenstall, in the form of Fitzpatrick's Temperance Bar, an original non-alcoholic pub that opened in 1890 as part of a network of temperance bars established to combat nineteenth-century alcoholism.

The bar takes its name from the Fitzpatricks, an Irish family of herbalists, and serves a range of herbal cordials including Dandelion & Burdock, Sarsaparilla and the rather Gothic-sounding Blood Tonic Cordial.

Website: www.fitzpatrickstemperancebar.co.uk
Address: 5 Bank St, Rawtenstall, Rossendale, BB4 6QS
Nearest station: Bolton

Play the Hood Game

For more than 700 years, the people of the North Lincolnshire village of Haxey have been playing the Hood Game, in which a huge and unstructured scrum aims to push the 'hood' – a leather tube – towards one of the four local pubs, which then gets to keep it until the next year.

The game – which roughly coincides with Old Christmas Day on 6 January – is based on the story of Lady de Mowbray, the wife of a local landowner, who, legend has it, lost her red hood when out riding, leaving thirteen farm workers to chase it around a field. The day is led by the Fool, who represents the man who caught the hood but was too shy to hand it back to Lady de Mowbray.

Website: www.isleofaxholme.net/haxey-hood.html
Address: The Carpenter's Arms, Newbigg, Westwoodside, DN9 2AT
Nearest station: Doncaster

Visit the Deep

Despite billing itself fairly meaninglessly as the world's only 'submarium', the Deep in Hull is an impressive aquarium. The building juts out over the waterfront, contains 2.5 million litres of water, and is home to more than 3,500 sea creatures.

The aquarium was opened in 2002 and boasts Europe's only pair of green sawfish, as well as eight other types of shark and a coral reef, teeming with tropical fish.

Website: www.thedeep.co.uk
Address: The Deep Aquarium, Tower St, Hull, HU1 4DP
Nearest station: Hull

Cross the Ironbridge

Celebrated by some as the birthplace of the Industrial Revolution, Ironbridge was once the most technologically advanced town in the world, after Abraham Darby began to use coke fuel in the smelting of iron there in 1709.

The 100-foot iron bridge from which the town takes its name was the world's first metal bridge. It was built by Darby's grandson in 1779 and proved to be a great influence on subsequent technology and architecture. The bridge is freely open to the public and a number of museums in the town tell the story of local industry.

Website: www.ironbridge.org.uk
Address: Museum of the Gorge, The Wharfage, Ironbridge TF8 7DQ
Nearest station: Wellington or Telford

Tour the HMS *Trincomalee*

The centrepiece of Hartlepool's Maritime Experience, a themed recreation of the town in the eighteenth century, HMS *Trincomalee* was built in Bombay, India, in 1817. It is the oldest British warship still afloat, and the second oldest floating ship in the world.

The ship sits in the town's Jackson Dock, where it arrived in 1987 for ten years of restoration following work as a training ship, and is now part of the National Historic Fleet, Core Collection.

Website: www.hms-trincomalee.co.uk
Address: Jackson Dock, Maritime Ave, Hartlepool, Cleveland TS24 0XZ
Nearest station: Hartlepool

Have Lunch at the Hartside Top Café

Known for its panoramic views and the steep bends that must be negotiated to get there, the Hartside Top Café is England's highest café, located on Hartside Pass on the A686 between Penrith and Alston in the North Pennines.

Particularly popular with cyclists and motorbikers, owing to its 1,904-foot altitude and the challenging route, the café is open on weekends during January, weather permitting.

Website: www.transportcafe.co.uk/hartsidetop.html
Address: Hartside Top Café, Alston, Cumbria, CA9 3BW
Nearest station: Penrith

Visit Bristol's M-Shed

Bristol's M-Shed is an interesting and informative museum of the city's history, opened in 2011. It was built in one of the alphabetically labelled transit sheds in the docks, hence its curious name, which was first given in the 1950s.

The museum offers a very interesting exploration of the culture and history of the city that is often considered the capital of the West Country.

Website: mshed.org
Address: Princes Wharf, Wapping Rd, Bristol, BS1 4RN
Nearest station: Bristol

FOLLOW *THE* MAYFLOWER TRAIL

Now remembered around the world as the founders of one of the first European settlements in North America, the Pilgrim Fathers began their lives in a quiet corner of the English countryside on the borders between Yorkshire, Lincolnshire and Derbyshire.

The Mayflower Trail visits various locations associated with the Pilgrims, including Babworth Church, where the religious separatism of the Pilgrim Fathers originated, led by the parson Richard Clyfton; Scrooby, where William Brewster held meetings of the separatist congregation at his manor house; and Gainsborough Old Hall, where John Smyth held meetings of his congregation.

Website: http://mayflowermaid.com/mayflower_trail_map
Address: Babworth All Saints Church, Bridle Path, Babworth, Nottinghamshire, DN22 7BP
Nearest station: Retford

Join the Kilmersdon Wassail

The Somerset village of Kilmersdon lies within cider-apple territory and takes its wassailing seriously, keen to ensure a good cider crop by blessing the apple trees in its Community Orchard.

The village, which is said to be home to the hill climbed by Jack and Jill in the nursery rhyme of the same name, crowns a Wassail Queen each year, and celebrates the season with music and Morris dancing.

Website: www.frome-tc.gov.uk
Address: Kilmersdon Village Hall, Kilmersdon, Somerset BA3 5TD
Nearest station: Frome

THINGS TO DO TODAY:

SEE THE ART OF THE PITMEN PAINTERS

Otherwise known as the Ashington Group, the Pitmen Painters were a group of working-class coal miners from Ashington in Northumberland who started meeting regularly in the 1930s as part of a Workers' Education Association group to study art appreciation, and who subsequently began painting their own works.

The results were seen by many as a uniquely insightful collection of working-class art, capturing aspects of life in Northern mining communities and leading to critically acclaimed exhibitions in Durham, London, Germany, the Netherlands and China. The group's pictures, reflecting life in their local community, are now on permanent exhibition at the Woodhorn Museum in Ashington.

Website: www.experiencewoodhorn.com
Address: Woodhorn Museum and Archives, Queen Elizabeth II Country Park, Ashington, Northumberland, NE63 9YF
Nearest station: Newcastle

Eat at the Crab & Lobster

An eccentrically decorated seventeenth-century thatched restaurant and pub at Asenby, near Thirsk in North Yorkshire, the Crab & Lobster specialises in good food in an interesting environment, with a treasure trove of antiques, including old advertising boards, fishing nets and characterful Marilyn Monroe-themed toilets.

The warm and cosy bar is perfect for a winter lunch, and the area's close connection to the North Sea coast means that seafood enjoys a strong presence on the menu.

Website: www.crabandlobster.co.uk
Address: Crab Manor Hotel, Dishforth, Asenby, North Yorks., YO7 3QL
Nearest station: Northallerton

Wander the Streets of Staithes

Known for its narrow cobbled streets and higgledy-piggledy cottages, the village of Staithes on the North Yorkshire coast was an important fishing port when a sixteen-year-old James Cook came here to work in a grocery shop in 1745.

The village now remembers Cook – who went on to become the famous explorer Captain Cook – in a heritage centre, and the village makes a good spot from which to explore the rugged coastline.

Website: www.staithes-town.info
Address: Staithes, North Yorkshire
Nearest station: Saltburn

Drink at Ye Olde Trip to Jerusalem

People have been gathering at Ye Olde Trip to Jerusalem for special events since at least the twelfth century, when it is believed that knights and supporters of Richard the Lionheart rested here before departing for Jerusalem to fight in the Third Crusade, hence the pub's name.

Built into the cliffs beneath Nottingham Castle, with the cellars and some of the rooms actually carved out from the rock, the pub is one of many that claim to be the oldest in England.

Website: www.triptojerusalem.com
Address: Brewhouse Yard, Nottingham, England NG1 6AD
Nearest station: Nottingham

Learn the History of Barrow Docks

An interesting museum exploring local history, the Dock Museum in Barrow-in-Furness, Cumbria, is located within a former dry dock, offering visitors an insight into the expansion of the industrial town, with a focus on shipbuilding and steel production.

The museum is a good starting place for those wishing to understand a modern-day town that is still shaped by its shipyards, which have continued to build submarines and other ships for the Royal Navy.

Website: www.dockmuseum.org.uk
Address: Dock Museum, North Road, Barrow-in-Furness, LA14 2PW
Nearest station: Barrow-in-Furness

Observe Holly Holy Day

In January 1644, at the height of the English Civil War, the Parliamentarian garrison at Nantwich in Cheshire was under siege, surrounded by Royalists forces. A Parliamentarian relief force marched south from Lancashire towards Nantwich, and the Battle of Nantwich began.

On 25 January 1644, the siege was finally lifted and the people of the town wore holly sprigs in their hats to celebrate. Since then, the day has been remembered as Holly Holy Day, and the soldiers of the Sealed Knot re-enactment organisation now come to the town each year in late January for a weekend's recreation of the battle.

Website: www.battleofnantwich.co.uk
Address: Nantwich, Cheshire
Nearest station: Nantwich

Visit the National Space Centre

The outskirts of Leicester may not be where you would expect to find the National Space Centre, but since 2001 it has indeed been based here, attracting a quarter of a million visitors each year.

The centre brings together a range of artefacts and exhibitions relating to space science and astronomy, including a 1970s Russian Soyuz spacecraft, a space suit worn by the first Briton in space, Helen Sharman, and a mock-up of the Columbus module built for the International Space Station.

Website: www.spacecentre.co.uk
Address: Exploration Dr., Leicester, LE4 5NS
Nearest station: Leicester

TAKE A TURKISH BATH IN HARROGATE

The Victorian Turkish Baths in Harrogate are an original part of the town's nineteenth-century Royal Baths complex, built to attract visitors to the spa town that has been known for its mineral waters since a spring was first discovered there by William Slingsby in 1571.

The restored Turkish Baths are one of only a handful of such surviving Victorian facilities, remaining true to their original grand Moorish design with Islamic arches and screens, walls of colourful glazed brickwork, painted ceilings and terrazzo floors, as well as a variety of steam rooms and hot rooms and a cool plunge pool.

Website: www.turkishbathsharrogate.co.uk
Address: Harrogate Turkish Baths & Health Spa, Parliament Street, Harrogate HG1 2WH
Nearest station: Harrogate

February

With the arrival of February, many hope spring is around the corner, but it still feels a lifetime away, as storm clouds and icy spells continue to dominate. However, although February is short, it is a month of change, and by the final week early daffodils become common in the South and the first lambs are born.

In Old English, February was called 'Solmonath' or 'the month of cakes', signifying offerings of cakes made to the gods; and it remains a month for food lovers, with bacon, pea soup and pancakes all traditional in the run up to Shrove Tuesday. The month is also a time for lovers, with Valentine's Day observed by couples, and ladies encouraged to propose in the event of a leap day at the end of the month.

Explore England's Oldest Museum

Opened in 1683 to house a collection donated to Oxford University by Elias Ashmole, Oxford's Ashmolean Museum is the oldest surviving museum in the country. The museum moved to its current location in 1845, and now attracts more than half a million visitors each year, displaying objects and art from around the world in its recently renovated galleries.

Officially called the Ashmolean Museum of Art and Archaeology, the museum houses a fascinating collection, including art by Pablo Picasso, Paul Cézanne, J M W Turner and Leonardo da Vinci, as well as Oliver Cromwell's death mask and Guy Fawkes' lantern.

Website: www.ashmolean.org
Address: Beaumont St, Oxford OX1 2PH
Nearest station: Oxford

See the Snowdrops at Fountains Abbey

Originally founded in 1132, Fountains Abbey stands in 800 acres of parkland and was once one of the richest religious houses in England. The abbey was dissolved in 1539 by Henry VIII, but it remains one of the largest and best preserved in England, and has been designated a World Heritage Site.

Today, the parkland around the abbey is known for its snowdrops, making early spring a special time to explore the ruins and the landscaped Georgian water garden. The presence of these flowers at the site dates back to the nineteenth century, when Earl de Grey – who owned the site – planted snowdrops to spell out his name along the River Skell.

Website: www.fountainsabbey.org.uk
Address: Fountains Abbey, Ripon HG4 3DY
Nearest station: Harrogate

TAKE A ROOFTOP BATH

The Thermae Spa at Bath is England's only naturally heated thermal spa, using hot springs that were discovered by **Prince Bladud in around 863 BC** and made famous by the Romans, who constructed a temple on their site.

The baths at Bath have been a popular spot for centuries, and even gave the Anglo-Saxon town its name. The Thermae Bath Spa is the latest in a long line of bath houses enjoyed by locals. Opened in 2006, it is crowned with an open-air rooftop pool with great views over the city.

Website: www.thermaebathspa.com
Address: The Hetling Pump Room, Hot Bath St, Bath BA1 1SJ
Nearest station: Bath

WATCH THE WORLD'S OLDEST PANCAKE RACE

Though it moves with Shrove Tuesday – usually in February but sometimes in March – the pancake race at Olney in Buckinghamshire is a rigid tradition, thought to be the world's oldest such event. It has taken place annually since 1445, when, legend has it, a townswoman who was late for the Shriving service forgot to put down her pan before running to church.

The annual pancake race, in which only women may compete, is still followed by a traditional Shriving service. Wearing traditional aprons and caps, and carrying a frying pan containing a real pancake, they set off just before noon and must toss their pancake once outside the Bull Inn before racing to the finish line at the church.

Website: www.olneyonline.com/Pancake-Race-History
Address: Olney High Street
Nearest station: Milton Keynes

Drink in the Pub where DNA was Discovered

In late February 1953, scientists Francis Crick and James Watson lunched at the Eagle pub in Cambridge and announced, 'We have discovered the secret of life.' They had identified DNA, and as the pub was where they had often discussed their research, it seemed a fitting spot for the announcement.

The Eagle dates back to c.1600, but is famous for its RAF bar, where the graffiti of Second World War pilots can be seen on the ceiling.

Website: www.gkpubs.co.uk/pubs-in-cambridge/eagle-pub
Address: Benet Street, Cambridge, CB2 3QN
Nearest station: Cambridge

Have a Bakewell Pudding at the Rutland Arms

Synonymous with the town of Bakewell in the Derbyshire Dales, the Bakewell Pudding is said to have been the result of a baking error by the cook at the Rutland Arms Hotel.

The story goes that a guest ordered a strawberry tart, but that the cook, instead of stirring the egg mixture into the pastry, poured it over the strawberry jam. The pudding was an instant success and soon became recognised as a trademark dish of the town.

Website: www.rutlandarmsbakewell.co.uk
Address: The Square, Bakewell, Derbyshire, DE45 1BT
Nearest station: Chesterfield or Buxton

Seek Shelter in Kents Cavern

Our ancient ancestors kept warm by building fires in the caves at Kents Cavern in Torbay, and it remains a shelter from the elements for people tens of thousands of years later.

A human jawbone found in the caves in 1927 has been dated to between 44,200 and 41,500 BP – the oldest human fossil in Britain – and earlier Neanderthal flint implements have also been found here, suggesting that the caves were occupied considerably earlier than that.

Website:: www.kents-cavern.co.uk
Address: 91 Ilsham Road, Torquay, Devon TQ1 2JF
Nearest station: Torquay

Eat Rhubarb in Wakefield

The rhubarb-producing area between the Yorkshire towns of Wakefield, Morley and Rothwell has for many years been known as the Rhubarb Triangle. Since the 1880s, the area has been the home of Yorkshire Forced Rhubarb, grown using a distinctive method first developed in the 1820s – indoors, under dark and warm conditions.

Though the days of special express rhubarb trains carrying tons of Yorkshire Forced Rhubarb for the markets of London have passed, rhubarb is still being grown in the Triangle. At the height of the season in February, Wakefield's annual Festival of Food, Drink and Rhubarb celebrates the year's harvest.

Website: www.therhubarbtrianglefarmshop.co.uk
Address: Green End Farm, Carlton, Wakefield, West Yorkshire WF3 3QR
Nearest station: Wakefield

Cycle the Snake Pass

Crossing a remote stretch of the A57 between Manchester and Sheffield, the Snake Pass has achieved legendary status among cyclists as one of only a few roads in England that can compete with the hill stages of Alpine cycling, regularly attracting adventurous cyclists on weekends and frequently featuring in the Tour of Britain.

The road switches between tight moorland bends and heavily forested sections around the Snake Pass Inn, and has a fearsome reputation with drivers and cyclists alike, as a result of its altitude, its questionable safety record and its frequent closures during inclement weather.

Website: www.snakepassinn.co.uk
Address: Snake Pass Inn, Snake Road, Bamford, Hope Valley, S33 0BJ
Nearest station: Bamford

Stand Beside the Angel of the North

Designed by Antony Gormley and erected in February 1998, the *Angel of the North* is an iconic sculpture standing twenty metres tall on the site of a former colliery baths beside the A1 near Gateshead. A car park on the A167 allows visitors wanting a closer look to stop and walk up to the Angel.

Unlike many pieces of public art, the *Angel of the North* has been a popular success, embraced by the people of the North East. Its roadside position – where it is seen by more than one person every second – makes it one of the most-viewed pieces of art in the world.

Website: www.angelofthenorth.org.uk
Address: Low Eighton, Gateshead, Tyne and Wear NE8 7UB
Nearest station: Newcastle

Ride the Middlesbrough Transporter Bridge

Carrying travellers across the River Tees for more than a century, the Middlesbrough Transporter Bridge spans 851 feet, making it the longest remaining bridge of its kind in the world. It was designed with sufficient height to allow sailing ships to pass underneath without having to remove their masts.

The bridge operates by carrying vehicles and passengers in a suspended gondola between Middlesbrough and Port Clarence every fifteen minutes for eighteen hours a day, and is so much part of local life that fireworks were launched from it as part of Middlesbrough's millennium celebrations.

Website: www.middlesbrough.gov.uk/index.aspx?articleid=1854
Address: Ferry Rd, Middlesbrough, TS2 1PL
Nearest station: Middlesbrough

Visit the Henry Moore Institute

Born in Castleford near Leeds, in 1898, and trained at the Leeds School of Art, Henry Moore was the most influential and famous sculptor of his generation.

The Henry Moore Institute in Leeds was established by the Henry Moore Foundation, the charity Moore himself set up before his death to promote sculpture and the visual arts, and hosts regular exhibitions and events at its building on The Headrow, in the centre of the city.

Website: www.henry-moore.org
Address: Dane Tree House, Perry Green, Much Hadham, SG10 6EE
Nearest station: Bishops Stortford

Scan the Stars at Jodrell Bank

Home to the enormous and instantly recognisable Lovell Telescope since 1957, Jodrell Bank is an important centre of English astronomy and has quietly been exploring the outer reaches of space from a field in the Cheshire countryside for more than fifty years.

The centre is open all year, though the crystal-clear skies of February make it a good time to attend stargazing events. It hosts regular events for all ages, and is home to a 35-acre arboretum with 2,000 species of trees and shrubs.

Website: www.jodrellbank.net
Address: Jodrell Bank Discovery Centre, Macclesfield, Cheshire, SK11 9DL
Nearest station: Macclesfield

Visit Sheffield Winter Garden

The largest urban greenhouse in Europe, the Winter Garden in Sheffield was opened in 2003 and offers a popular escape from the elements, as well as an indoor garden that is home to more than 2,000 plants from around the world.

The garden features 150 species of plants beneath its twenty-one-metre-high ceiling, including palms from Central America, Madagascar and China.

Website: www.sheffield.gov.uk
Address: 90 Surrey St, South Yorkshire, Sheffield S1 2LH
Nearest station: Sheffield

Gaze Out from the Spot that Inspired Bram Stoker's Dracula

The first monastery at Whitby was founded in AD 657, and the walls of its imposing eleventh-century Gothic successor still stand proudly on the hill above the town. It was among the windswept ruins that Bram Stoker drew inspiration for his 1897 novel *Dracula*.

In the novel, a Russian ship is wrecked off the coast of Whitby during a fierce storm. Looking out to the North Sea from the Abbey on a wild day, it is easy to see what Stoker found so inspiring, and why so many *Dracula* fans visit the spot to this day.

Website: www.whitbyabbey.co.uk
Address: Abbey Lane, Whitby, North Yorkshire YO22 4JT
Nearest station: Sheffield

THINGS TO DO TODAY:

SPEND A NIGHT AT THE HOUSE IN THE CLOUDS

The House in the Clouds in Thorpeness, Suffolk, was built by the Braithwaite Engineering Company in 1923 as a water tower. It provided water to the village by pumping it from the mill well and distributing it by gravity, in what is a rather flat part of the country.

The building was customised to give it the appearance of a house, or very tall cottage, although it continued to be used as a water tower until 1963, when a mains water supply was connected. In 1989, work began to convert it into a five-floor house, which is available for holiday lets today.

Website: www.houseintheclouds.co.uk
Address: Uplands Rd, Thorpeness, Leiston IP16 4NQ
Nearest station: Saxmundham

Become a Codebreaker at Bletchley Park

During the Second World War, Bletchley Park in Buckinghamshire was at the front line of Britain's struggle against the Germans, and at the height of the war, more than 10,000 people worked away secretly in various huts, often unaware of how exactly their work was helping the war effort.

Since 1993, Bletchley Park has been open to the public as a tribute to the codebreakers who broke the German cypher systems, Enigma and Lorenz, telling the story of their incredible feats of military intelligence, which are estimated to have cut the war short by up to two years.

Website: www.bletchleypark.org.uk
Address: The Mansion, Bletchley Park, Milton Keynes, MK3 6EB
Nearest station: Bletchley

Drink the Waters of Buxton Spring

Buxton has been famous for its spring water for centuries, and the Peak District town still takes great pride in its waters. At St Ann's Well, close to the centre of Buxton, the celebrated waters come gushing freely out of the mouth of a fierce bronze lion.

The current well casing was installed in around 1940, at a site on which wells have stood since Roman times, as a tribute to Councillor Emelie Dorothy Bounds. Locals often stop to fill up bottles of the water from the well, which is decorated with a statue of St Ann and child, and whose water is said to have health-giving properties.

Website: http://www.peakdistrictinformation.com/towns/buxton.php
Address: Opposite the Crescent, Buxton
Nearest station: Buxton

Sit Beside the Fire at the Warren House Inn

Whatever the weather outside, visitors to the Warren House Inn can always be sure of a warm welcome, with a fire that has burned continuously in the hearth since 1845. The Inn cuts a lonely figure in the middle of Dartmoor, on what was once a packhorse route serving local tin mines.

The Warren House was built in the eighteenth century on the site of an earlier pub. Where once it served passing miners, today you are more likely to find walkers enjoying the local scenery and sheltering from a rain shower.

Website: www.warrenhouseinn.co.uk
Address: The Warren House Inn, Postbridge, Devon, PL20 6TA
Nearest station: Okehampton

See the Long Man of Wilmington

A mysterious figure on the slopes of Windover Hill in Sussex, the Long Man of Wilmington was first recorded in 1710, in a drawing made by a surveyor called John Rowley.

Though no one knows the origin of the figure, he continues to capture the imagination, with local neo-druids gathering at the Long Man to mark Imbolc, one of the eight Pagan festivals of the year, which usually falls in early February.

Website: www.sussexpast.co.uk/properties-to-discover/the-long-man
Address: Signposted on A27, 2 miles west of the junction with A22 at Polegate
Nearest station: Berwick or Polegate

Walk Around Beachy Head

Britain's tallest chalk cliffs are found at Beachy Head, which rises sharply from Eastbourne towards its highest point before falling away to the west towards Birling Gap and the Seven Sisters Country Park.

Despite icy winds, February at Beachy Head can be very rewarding, with stunning sunsets over the sea to the south. For those who can manage not to get sidetracked by the pubs en route, a circular walk from Eastbourne to East Dean, via Beachy Head and Birling Gap, makes a fulfilling day out.

Website: www.beachyhead.org.uk
Address: East Dean, East Sussex
Nearest station: Eastbourne

Eat Scallops in Rye

While the number of boats at many South Coast ports has gradually dwindled and died, the Sussex town of Rye maintains a small fishing fleet of twenty to thirty boats, keeping alive a history of fishing in a town that was one of two 'Antient Townes' allied to the medieval Cinque Ports.

To support its local fishing industry, the town now holds its annual Rye Bay Scallop Festival, with special menus in eateries around the town, and talks, markets and tours with a scallop theme.

Website: scallop.org.uk
Address: Venues throughout Rye, early February
Nearest station: Rye (Sussex)

See the Petrifying Well

Since at least the seventeenth century, the well at Mother Shipton's Cave – the legendary birthplace of the Yorkshire prophetess – has been recognised for a unique quality: the ability to turn almost any object into stone over the course of a few months.

One of England's oldest visitor attractions, the well is found at Knaresborough in Yorkshire, and its mysterious properties appear to work on anything from a shoe to a teddy bear, the result of unusually high mineral content in the waters that flow over offerings left there.

Website: www.mothershipton.co.uk/petrifying-well
Address: Prophecy Lodge, High Bridge, Knaresborough, North Yorks., HG5 8DD
Nearest station: Knaresborough

SEE THE HOUSE THAT INSPIRED BEATRIX POTTER

In 1905, using her inheritance and royalties earned from her first few books, Beatrix Potter acquired Hill Top, a farm at Near Sawrey in the Lake District, as an escape from London. Potter's love affair with the Lakes would see her remain closely attached to the area until she died in the village nearly forty years later.

Near Sawrey inspired many of Potter's later books, with Hill Top providing a fictional home for Samuel Whiskers and Tom Kitten, Esthwaite Water the stomping ground of Mr Jeremy Fisher, and the Tower Bank Arms featured in The Tale of Jemima Puddle-Duck. Hill Top is open to visitors, preserved exactly as Potter left it.

Website: www.nationaltrust.org.uk/hill-top/
Address: Hill Top, Near Sawrey, Ambleside, LA22 0LF
Nearest station: Windermere

Take the Mersey Ferry

Vessels have been crossing the Mersey since at least the twelfth century, when they began as a way to transport Benedictine monks from the priory at Birkenhead. Today, ferries continue to ply the route between Seacombe terminal and Liverpool's Pier Head, taking commuters in the morning and evening and leisure travellers on longer cruises during the rest of the day.

While numbers of passengers have declined with the opening of the Mersey Railway Tunnel in 1886, the Queensway Tunnel in 1934 and the Kingsway Tunnel in 1971, the ferries have survived and continue to transport up to 650,000 passengers each year.

Website: www.merseyferries.co.uk
Address: Woodside, Merseyside, Birkenhead, Merseyside CH41 6DU
Nearest station: Birkenhead Hamilton Square

Stand at Britain's Most Easterly Point

Ness Point in Lowestoft is the most easterly point in Great Britain, a fact marked by the Euroscope, a large circular installation designed by John Wylson and installed in the 1990s, showing distances to various points in Europe.

The point is roughly 470 miles from Dunnet Head, the most northerly point in mainland Britain, and 350 miles from the Lizard, the most southerly point.

Website: www.ness-point.co.uk
Address: Lowestoft, Suffolk
Nearest station: Lowestoft

Take Tea at Lucknam Park

The Lucknam Park Hotel, situated in 500 acres of Wiltshire parkland outside Bath, is a lovely spot for an afternoon tea. The house was built under the watchful eye of eighteenth-century Bristol merchant James Wallis, who created the estate we see today.

High tea – complete with scones, cakes, sandwiches and a choice of teas – is served in the drawing room, beside a crackling log fire, in a relaxed and friendly atmosphere that allows visitors to escape from the cold outside.

Website: www.lucknampark.co.uk
Address: Lucknam Park Hotel & Spa, Bath, Wiltshire, SN14 8AZ
Nearest station: Bath

Visit Burgh Castle

Burgh Castle is a third-century Roman fort overlooking the River Waveney in the Norfolk Broads. There is evidence to suggest the fort was Gariannonum, one of nine forts referred to in Notitia Dignitatum – a rare surviving document from the Roman administration – and constructed by the Saxon Shore military command to defend against Saxon raids in East Anglia.

One of the best-preserved Roman monuments in England, the castle is open to the public and free to visit. It is owned by the Norfolk Archaeological Trust, with its walls under the care of English Heritage.

Website: www.english-heritage.org.uk/daysout/properties/burgh-castle
Address: Butt Lane, Burgh Castle, Norfolk, NR31 9PZ
Nearest station: Great Yarmouth

March

Primroses and violets emerge in the hedgerows as the vernal equinox approaches, marking half way to summer. However, despite the change, March can offer one of the widest variations in weather, with Anglo-Saxons referring to the month as 'Hlyd monath' or 'stormy month', and farmers declaring, "If March comes in like a lion, it will go out like a lamb" – meaning early wintry weather should make way for spring by the end.

Prior to 1752, the English year began on 25 March, and signs of renewal are seen throughout the month, with the planting of spring crops and later in the month carpets of woodland bluebells appearing. With warmer weather, and lengthening days, it's time to get yourself up and about in the great outdoors.

EXPLORE EXETER'S UNDERGROUND PASSAGES

Originally constructed in the fourteenth and fifteenth centuries in order to transport fresh drinking water into the city, Exeter's underground passages were still in use until 1857, when they were partly damaged by the building of a new railway cutting. By the turn of the twentieth century, the passages were all but forgotten, but happily, in the 1930s, they found a new lease of life when they were opened to the public for tours.

Despite a brief break during the Second World War, when they were used as a bomb shelter for up to 300 people, the tunnels have been open to the public ever since. A new visitor centre tells their fascinating subterranean secret history.

Website: www.exeter.gov.uk/passages
Address: Exeter City Council, 2 Paris Street, Exeter, Devon, EX1 1GA
Nearest station: Exeter

Visit Dove Cottage and Dora's Field

The former home of the influential English Romantic poet William Wordsworth, Dove Cottage is now a museum to his life and work. Wordsworth lived at the cottage with his wife from 1799 to 1808 and produced some of his most important works here, using a bright upstairs bedroom as his sitting room, as the natural light made it especially amenable for reading and writing.

In daffodil season the short walk to Dora's Field in the neighbouring village of Rydal is a must. Wordsworth bought the land next to St Mary's Church and planned to build a house there for his daughter, Dora. However, when Dora died in 1847, the family decided instead to plant hundreds of daffodils in her memory, a tradition that continues today.

Website: wordsworth.org.uk/visit/dove-cottage.html
Address: Dove Cottage, Town End, Grasmere, Ambleside LA22 9SH
Nearest station: Windermere

See the Rollright Stones

A collection of three Neolithic and Bronze Age megalithic monuments close to the small village of Little Rollright ('Rollright' is believed to derive from the Old English 'Hrolla landriht', or 'Land of Hrolla') on the borders of Oxfordshire and Warwickshire, the Rollright Stones are remembered in folklore as the remains of a regional king and his supporters, who aimed to conquer England but were turned to stone by a witch.

The stones consist of a Neolithic Stone Circle known as the King's Men, a 5,000-year-old burial chamber called the Whispering Knights and a single Bronze Age monolith standing fifty yards away on the opposite side of the road, known as the King Stone.

Website: www.rollrightstones.co.uk
Address: Follow the uphill footpath from the village of Long Compton
Nearest station: Moreton-in-Marsh

Seek Sustenance in Bray

The Berkshire village of Bray could fairly be described as the culinary capital of England, containing two of the country's four restaurants with three Michelin stars: Heston Blumenthal's Fat Duck; and the Waterside Inn, founded in 1972 by Michel and Albert Roux.

In addition, Blumenthal's pubs, the Hinds Head and the Crown, can be found in the heart of the village, meaning that visitors can be sure of a good feed – as long as they can secure a table.

Website: www.windsor-berkshire.co.uk/bray
Address: The Hinds Head, High Street, Bray, SL6 2AB
Nearest station: Windsor

Explore the Battlements of Berwick

Built in 1558 to defend a town that had been a flashpoint of Anglo-Scottish relations, changing hands thirteen times in two centuries, the substantial walls at Berwick-upon-Tweed were one of the biggest financial investments of the reign of Queen Elizabeth I, built to an Italian design to ensure full protection against potential invaders.

Though the walls are very grand – and make a pleasant place to walk around and appreciate the absorbing frontier town – the expense was ultimately futile: the Scots never attacked. Within fifty years, James VI of Scotland had crossed the Tweed at Berwick to become King James I of England, and the Union of the Crowns turned the walls into an attractive folly.

Website: www.visitnorthumberland.com/historic-sites/
Address: Town Walls, Berwick-upon-Tweed, Northumberland, TD15 1BN
Nearest station: Berwick-upon-Tweed

Remember William Wilberforce

In the heart of Hull's Old Town, the building now called the Wilberforce House Museum was, in 1759, the birthplace of William Wilberforce, one of the city's most celebrated residents and the man who led the movement to abolish slavery.

The museum recounts the history of the transatlantic slave trade and the movement to abolish it, as well as presenting the story of the great man through contemporary artefacts from his life.

Website: www.hullcc.gov.uk/museumcollections
Address: 25 High Street, Hull HU1 1NQ
Nearest station: Hull

Visit Great Coxwell Barn

Great Coxwell Barn is a huge fourteenth-century tithe barn in the Oxfordshire village of Great Coxwell, which once stored the produce of a monastic farm owned by Beaulieu Abbey in Hampshire.

A vast space, with walls of Cotswold stone and a stone-tiled roof supported by a network of wooden beams, it feels more like a cathedral than a barn, and has long drawn appreciative visitors, including, in the late nineteenth century, local luminary William Morris.

Website: www.nationaltrust.org.uk/great-coxwell-barn
Address: Great Coxwell, Faringdon, Oxfordshire SN7 7LZ
Nearest station: Swindon

Experience Life in a Victorian Workhouse

While many historic buildings are showcases of English aristocracy, this cannot be said for The Workhouse in Southwell, Nottinghamshire, built in 1824 and one of the most complete Victorian workhouses in existence.

A Grade II*-listed building, the Workhouse offers a grim insight into how previous societies dealt with poor people, allowing visitors to explore the rooms in which inmates lived and worked.

Website: www.nationaltrust.org.uk/workhouse-southwell
Address: Upton Road, Southwell, NG25 0PT
Nearest station: Fiskerton

Mark St Piran's Day

The festival of St Piran, Cornwall's patron saint, is honoured across the South Western county on the days around 5 March, and Bodmin holds an annual St Piran's Day procession, with speeches, songs, dances and plays, to celebrate the history of Cornwall.

Elsewhere, the day – which was historically observed by Cornish tin miners – is marked by a St Piran Play on Perran Sands near Perranporth, and processions through the streets of Penzance and Truro.

Website: www.stpiransday.com
Address: Bodmin, Cornwall
Nearest station: Bodmin Parkway

Drink at the Turk's Head, Penzance

The Turk's Head claims to be among Cornwall's oldest pubs, dating its foundation to 1233, when a Turkish invasion of Penzance took place, said to have been directed from Jerusalem as part of the Crusades. The pub has been in continuous use since then, with only a brief pause after it was partially burned down as part of a Spanish invasion in the sixteenth century.

Given its close association with Cornish history, it is unsurprising that the Turk's Head was traditionally popular with smugglers and pirates, and a secret underground tunnel leading from the harbour is said to have been used to transport contraband, helping to maintain its popularity as a smuggler's haunt.

Website: www.turksheadpenzance.co.uk
Address: 49 Chapel St, Penzance, Cornwall TR18 4AF
Nearest station: Penzance

Spend a Night at Britain's Highest Pub

The Tan Hill Inn, 1,732 feet up in the Yorkshire Dales above Richmond, is Britain's highest pub. An inn is thought to have stood on Tan Hill since Tudor times, and the current pub dates from the seventeenth century, when it saw increased trade due to coal mining, which once took place on Tan Hill.

Today, the pub attracts a mixture of walkers, tourists and hardy locals, with rooms filled with guests on lively evenings and occasional music nights by the fire. In the company of a menagerie of lambs and other animals, and well insulated from the wild and windy weather outside, in winter the pub is often completely cut off from the outside world.

Website: www.tanhillinn.com
Address: Tan Hill, Reeth, Richmond, Swaledale, North Yorkshire, DL11 6ED
Nearest station: Darlington

Enter the World Poohsticks Championships

Since 1984, the sport of Poohsticks, immortalised by A A Milne in *The House at Pooh Corner*, has become a competitive event at Day's Lock near Dorchester-on-Thames. The rules of Poohsticks are very simple: a stick is dropped on one side of a bridge and, as the current takes it under the bridge, the first one to spot their stick on the other side is crowned the winner.

The annual competition – now held in March – was begun by the lock keeper, Lynn David, and frequently attracts more than 1,000 people.

Website: www.pooh-sticks.com
Address: Day's Lock, River Thames in Oxfordshire
Nearest station: Didcot Parkway

Go Cycling in the New Forest

Hampshire's New Forest has been woodland ever since the end of the last Ice Age, largely owing its continued existence to William the Conqueror, who chose it as his royal hunting forest in the eleventh century.

The forest is now a National Park covering more than 200 square miles, and boasts a fine network of cycle paths. Bicycles can be hired from Country Lanes cycle hire, which has a depot right beside the railway station in the heart of the forest at Brockenhurst, so there is no need to bring a car.

Website: www.countrylanes.co.uk
Address: Country Lanes, The Railway Station, Brockenhurst SO42 7TW
Nearest station: Brockenhurst

Stay at Tixall Gatehouse

The last remaining part of a grand estate that once stood in fields outside Stafford, the impressive Elizabethan Tixall Gatehouse witnessed the arrival of Mary, Queen of Scots, when she was imprisoned at Tixall Hall in the 1580s.

By the 1950s, following the demolition of the house, the gatehouse roof had fallen in and the building was all but ruined. Fortunately, it was saved by the Landmark Trust in the 1970s, and is now available to rent for holidays, with its distinctive turrets acting as characterful cabin-like bedrooms.

Website: www.landmarktrust.org.uk
Address: Tixall Gatehouse, Near Stafford, Staffordshire
Nearest station: Stafford

Eat Cheddar in Cheddar

The only business in Cheddar still making the famous cheese with which it shares its name, the Cheddar Gorge Cheese Company continues to make cheese in the traditional way.

The company has a viewing gallery, where visitors are invited to watch skilled cheese-makers making real Cheddar, with guides on hand to answer questions about its manufacture – and of course there's a free taster session afterwards.

Website: www.cheddargorgecheeseco.co.uk
Address: The Cliffs, Cheddar, Somerset, BS27 3QA
Nearest station: Weston-super-Mare

Step Inside the Birmingham Back-to-Backs

Built in the 1840s, the Birmingham Back-to-Backs at 50–54 Inge Street and 55–63 Hurst Street are the last remaining court of back-to-back houses in Birmingham, typical of the low-quality working-class housing that characterised areas of the Midlands and the North from the Industrial Revolution until the Second World War.

Restored by the Birmingham Conservation Trust, and owned by the National Trust, the houses – built back to back, around a central courtyard – are open to the public for tours, providing an insight into what life was like for those who lived in them from the 1840s right up until the 1970s.

Website: www.nationaltrust.org.uk/birmingham-back-to-backs/
Address: 55-63 Hurst Street/50-54 Inge Street, Birmingham, B5 4TE
Nearest station: Birmingham

ENTER A 'SECRET' NUCLEAR BUNKER

A subterranean maze of rooms and corridors, built during the Cold War by a government preparing for the possibility of nuclear war, Kelvedon Hatch bunker once offered an escape for up to 600 military and civilian personnel, around 100 feet beneath a field in rural Essex.

Originally constructed as part of an RAF air-defence project, the bunker was redesignated as one of the country's regional seats of government, from which the recovery mission would be directed in the event of nuclear war. After the end of the Cold War, the government decided that it no longer required the bunker and it is now open to the public as a museum.

Website: www.secretnuclearbunker.com
Address: Kelvedon Hatch, Crown Buildings, Kelvedon Hall Lane, Kelvedon Hatch, CM14 5TL
Nearest station: Brentwood and Shenfield

WALK TO THE NEEDLES HEADLAND

Probably the most dramatic landscape on the Isle of Wight, the chalk cliffs that run from Freshwater Bay over Tennyson Down to the Needles Battery are an inspirational place, once walked daily by Alfred, Lord Tennyson, who described the fresh salt air as 'worth sixpence a pint'.

A monument at the top of what is now called Tennyson Down remembers the poet, and a fine walk continues along the cliff tops to the Needles Battery, where the cliffs fall away into an inaccessible group of chalk stacks, at the end of which stands the iconic Needles lighthouse.

Website: www.nationaltrust.org.uk/needles-and-tennyson-down
Address: Needles Old Battery, West Highdown, Alum Bay, Isle of Wight, PO39 0JH
Nearest station: Yarmouth

See the White Horse at Uffington

One of the most impressive of the white-chalk horses that adorn the chalk hillsides of England, the Uffington White Horse is found in Oxfordshire, overlooking a beautiful valley now known as the Vale of the White Horse. The horse sits just below Uffington Castle, a hill fort with which it is thought to be associated, and close to an ancient track known as the Ridgeway.

No one is quite sure how old the mysterious chalk horse is, with written records only dating back as far as the twelfth century. While some believe that it dates from the Iron Age, others suggest that it was constructed to celebrate King Alfred's victories over the invading Danes in the ninth century.

Website: www.nationaltrust.org.uk/white-horse-hill
Address: Ridgeway, Whitehorse Hill, Uffington, Oxfordshire
Nearest station: Swindon

Ride the Settle to Carlisle Railway

The Settle to Carlisle Railway is one of England's great railway routes, passing through seventy-two miles of beautiful countryside and crossing stunning viaducts at Ribblehead, Smardale, Dent Head and Artengill. March is one of the best times of year to ride the line, with improved spring weather but still only a light covering of leaves on trees, offering better views.

The line was completed in 1876, with hundreds of the 6,000 men who worked on it by hand losing their lives during construction. The line narrowly avoided closure in the 1970s and 1980s, but remains open to mainline trains, and also occasional steam-train tours from private companies when capacity allows.

Website: www.settle-carlisle.co.uk
Address: Settle, North Yorkshire, BD24
Nearest station: Settle and Carlisle

WATCH A FILM AT THE KINEMA IN THE WOODS

Found in a predictably leafy setting on the outskirts of Woodhall Spa in Lincolnshire, the Kinema in the Woods began life as a sports pavilion in the grounds of a grand hotel. When the hotel burned down on Easter Sunday 1920, it was sold and the pavilion converted into a cinema, which opened in 1922.

The cinema remained in the hands of Major Allport – who undertook the original conversion – until 1973, and still retains its vintage charm, with one of very few changes being the addition of a second screen in 1994. It remains open daily to film enthusiasts, and is the only cinema in the country still to use rear projection, due to the height of its roof.

Website: www.thekinemainthewoods.co.uk
Address: Coronation Road, Woodhall Spa, Lincolnshire LN10 6QD
Nearest station: Metheringham

See the Wellington Monument

Rising 175 feet on a hillside overlooking the village of Wellington, Somerset, the Wellington Monument was erected to celebrate the Iron Duke's victory at Waterloo in 1815.

The Monument has been cared for by the National Trust since 1934, and its design is said to draw inspiration from the shape of both an Egyptian obelisk and that of a bayonet used by Wellington's armies.

Website: http://cmsen.eghn.org/wellingtonmonument
Address: Tourist Information Centre, 30 Fore Street, Wellington, TA21 8AQ
Nearest station: Taunton

Ride the Volk's Electric Railway

The world's oldest operating electric railway, Brighton's Volk's Electric Railway was opened in 1883. The railway takes its name from inventor Magnus Volk, the British-born son of a German clockmaker who was responsible for its creation.

The railway still runs every summer from the aquarium to the rocky outcrop at Black Rock, beside what is now Brighton Marina.

Website: www.volkselectricrailway.co.uk
Address: 285 Madeira Drive, Brighton, East Sussex, BN2 1EN
Nearest station: Brighton

See the Harringworth Viaduct

Stretching nearly three-quarters of a mile across the valley of the River Welland between Harringworth in Northamptonshire and Seaton in Rutland, the Harringworth Viaduct was completed in 1878.

Consisting of eighty-two arches, each spanning forty feet, the viaduct dominates the valley and is an impressive testament to the construction of the Victorian age. It has been awarded Grade II-listed status, and is estimated to include around 30 million bricks.

Website: www.theheritagetrail.co.uk/industrial/harringworth_viaduct.htm
Address: Rutland, Welland Valley
Nearest station: Oakham

Explore Blue John Cavern

Derbyshire's Blue John Cavern is actually a series of spectacular caverns, which are still a centre for the mining of rare Blue John stone, first mined by the Romans 2,000 years ago and found as far away as the ruins of Pompeii.

Today, the caverns are open daily to the public for tours. Visitors can explore the various caverns and learn about the stunning discoveries that have been made here over the past two millennia.

Website: www.bluejohn-cavern.co.uk
Address: Blue John Cavern, Mam Tor Castleton, Derbyshire, S33 8WA
Nearest station: Edale

Walk in a Rainforest

Opened in 1993, the Living Rainforest in Berkshire was a project led by philanthropist Keith Bromley to convert a former orchid nursery into an educational resource, allowing people to step inside a real rainforest without leaving England.

Now run by an independent charity and open all year round, the Living Rainforest brings together the plants, animals, sights and sounds of a rainforest environment to teach people about the importance of rainforest ecosystems and enable them to experience what a real rainforest is like.

Website: www.livingrainforest.org
Address: Hampstead Norreys, Thatcham,
West Berkshire RG18 0TN
Nearest station: Thatcham

Stay at Holbeck Ghyll

Commanding dramatic views across Windermere and ever-changing skies, Holbeck Ghyll was the nineteenth-century hunting lodge of Lord Lonsdale, and is now run as a small country-house hotel, boasting twenty-one rooms, a Michelin-starred restaurant and a spa.

Set in eighteen acres of private woodland and gardens, the hotel is right at the heart of the Lake District, with a homely style and walks right from the front door. Excellent facilities and a well-stocked wine cellar make it a pleasant place to be whatever weather the Cumbrian springtime throws at you.

Website: www.holbeckghyll.com
Address: Holbeck Ghyll, Holbeck Lane, Windermere, Cumbria, LA23 1LU
Nearest station: Windermere

Walk along Devil's Dyke

Stretching through seven and a half miles of rural Cambridgeshire, Devil's Dyke – supposedly created by the Devil's fiery tail trailing behind him as he was chased away by villagers from a wedding he had gate-crashed – is an important earthwork, constructed by the Anglo-Saxons.

Thought to have been used to delineate an important tribal boundary, the Dyke consists of a bank up to eleven metres tall beside a deep ditch, and could have been used for defensive purposes. Today, it offers great views over the surrounding countryside and a decent walk, with plenty of wildlife en route.

Website: www.nationaltrust.org.uk/devils-dyke/
Address: South Downs, near Brighton
Nearest station: Brighton

Watch the Boat Race

Usually taking place on the last Saturday in March, but occasionally on the first Saturday in April, the Boat Race between Oxford and Cambridge Universities has been held since March 1829, when Cambridge sent a challenge out to the Oxford boys to see who was best at rowing.

The annual race takes place over four miles and 374 yards, watched by up to 250,000 spectators along the banks of the Thames in London between Putney and Mortlake, and is one of the oldest sporting events in the world.

Website: http://theboatrace.org
Address: Putney Embankment to The Ship in Mortlake
Nearest station: Various along route

Explore Broomhill Sculpture Gardens

Set in the heart of the North Devon countryside near Barnstaple, the Broomhill Sculpture Park sits in ten acres of gardens and woodland, in the valley beneath the Broomhill Art Hotel. The park holds over 300 sculptures by 60-plus sculptors.

As well as the interesting artistic creations set in terraces beneath the hotel, the park is also known for its National Sculpture Prize, which offers an annual prize fund for ambitious and experimental sculptures; the shortlisted entries of which are exhibited in the grounds at Broomhill.

Website: www.broomhillart.co.uk/sculpturegardens
Address: Muddiford, Barnstaple, North Devon EX31 4EX
Nearest station: Barnstaple

VISIT 'ENGLAND'S FIRST SEASIDE RESORT'

Claimed by locals as England's first seaside resort, Scarborough had been an important town since the thirteenth century – when merchants came from around Europe for the six-week Scarborough Fair – but it was not until the seventeenth century, when a stream of acidic water was discovered, that the town was reborn as Scarborough Spa and began to attract visitors as a seaside resort.

Scarborough was transformed once more in 1845, when both the railway to York and the first hotel opened, followed in 1867 by the Grand Hotel, one of the largest in the world. The town has managed to avoid many of the issues of decline that have threatened other resorts and is still a popular destination, particularly with older crowds.

Website: www.scarboroughgrandhotel.co.uk
Address: St Nicholas Cliff, Scarborough, North Yorkshire, UK
Nearest station: Scarborough

April

April opens with tricks: its first day is marked as
'the day of fools', and practical jokes are played by
friends and families, as they have been for centuries.
Another ancient celebration, St George's Day, falls
on 23rd April, and whilst England doesn't celebrate
its saint with the vigour of its neighbours, crowds
flock to Stratford-upon-Avon for a twin celebration
with William Shakespeare's birthday.

Spring continues to gather pace, with dandelions,
daisies and primroses blooming, the arrival of the first
swallows and the first hearing of the cuckoo, which
traditionally begins to sing on St Tiburtius' Day,
14 April. However, April can be a month of deceptive
weather, known for its showers and also for its potential
to revert to wintry cold by those who warn, 'Never
trust an April sunshine'.

SEE THE MAPPA MUNDI

The Hereford Mappa Mundi at Hereford Cathedral is a fascinating map dating from around 1285, showing the world as it was seen in medieval times. Drawn on calf skin by Richard of Haldingham and Lafford, the map places Jerusalem at the centre, with the British Isles at its outer edges.

The map displays only what was known by Richard and his contemporaries, reaching as far as the River Ganges in India, the Nile in Africa and Norway and the Caspian Sea to the North, with strange beasts and creatures beyond. The neighbouring Chained Library – a unique collection of books dating back as far as the eighth century – is also open to the public.

Website: www.herefordcathedral.org/visit-us/mappa-mundi-1
Address: Hereford Cathedral, 5 College Cloisters, Cathedral Close, Hereford, HR1 2NG
Nearest station: Hereford

See a Prison Built for French and American Prisoners of War

Constructed to incarcerate French prisoners during the Napoleonic Wars, Dartmoor Prison sits at the centre of Southern England's last great wilderness, and is still in use as a prison today.

The on-site museum tells the story of the prison, which also held American prisoners of war during the War of 1812, while the shop sells benches and garden ornaments made by current inmates.

Website: www.dartmoor-prison.co.uk
Address: HMP Dartmoor, Yelverton, Devon PL20 6RR
Nearest station: Gunnislake

Spend a Night in a Gypsy Caravan

Situated in the heart of rural Herefordshire, close to the River Wye, Wriggles Brook is a B&B with a difference, offering accommodation in three traditional Romany bowtop wagons, all of them over 100 years old.

Clean linen, hot showers and a full breakfast are provided – as well as a few modern conveniences such as lights, power points and a radiator – but otherwise guests are set free to enjoy a traditional campfire and Gypsy griddle pan, and the peace and quiet of the countryside.

Website: wrigglesbrook.co.uk
Address: 2 Brookside, Hoarwithy, Herefordshire HR2 6QJ
Nearest station: Hereford

Visit the Bentley Wildfowl and Motor Museum

In the heart of rural Sussex, Bentley House is home to a twenty-three-acre wildfowl reserve and a motor museum containing scores of classic vehicles. Acquired by Gerald and Mary Askew in 1937, the estate was opened to the public in 1978.

Alongside the reserve and museum, the house and gardens are also open to visitors and include an adventure playground, a tea room and even a miniature railway.

Website: bentley.org.uk/
Address: Bentley Country Park, Halland, East Sussex, BN8 5AF
Nearest station: Uckfield

Drink at the Crooked House

Found at the end of a leafy lane in Gornalwood on the outskirts of Dudley, the Crooked House was first built in 1765 as a farmhouse, and later became a public house known as the Siden House, supposedly owing its name to the Black Country dialect, in which 'siden' means crooked.

The reason for its crookedness is mining that took place in the area during the nineteenth century, causing subsidence and threatening the very existence of the pub by the 1940s. Fortunately, it was saved by Wolverhampton and Dudley Breweries, who reinforced the building with supporting buttresses and girders.

Website: www.thecrooked-house.co.uk
Address: Coppice Mill Lane, Himley Road, Himley, Staffordshire DY3 4DA
Nearest station: Dudley

Learn About the Gurkhas

Nepalese Gurkha forces have been serving alongside the British since the days of the East India Company, having impressed with their resistance during the Gurkha War of 1814–16. In a unique agreement between the United Kingdom, India and Nepal, a number of Gurkhas remained serving with the British after independence in 1947.

This meant that – having already served in both the First and Second World Wars – some Gurkha troops have continued to serve in conflicts in the Falkland Islands, Kosovo, Bosnia, East Timor, Iraq and Afghanistan. Their service is remembered in the Gurkha Museum at the Peninsula Barracks in Winchester.

Website: www.thegurkhamuseum.co.uk
Address: Peninsula Barracks, Romsey Road, Winchester SO23 8TS
Nearest station: Winchester

See the Bluebells in Foxley Wood

April is a colourful time in the woodlands of England, as bluebells spring up, taking advantage of thin leaf canopies to soak up much-needed sunshine. Foxley Wood, the largest area of ancient woodland in Norfolk, is a particularly fine place to see them.

Foxley Wood was recorded in the Domesday Book but it was already well established by the time the Normans arrived, with some parts known to be over 6,000 years old. The wood is known for its wide rides, created to allow the movement of felled timber, which make wonderful paths far into the woodland and allow the bluebells more space to grow.

Website: www.friendsoffoxley.co.uk
Address: Foxley Village, Norfolk
Nearest station: Norwich

Celebrate Shakespeare's Birthday

The town of Stratford-upon-Avon is fiercely proud of its son, William Shakespeare, and the most hearty of celebrations of the Bard take place on the nearest weekend to his birthday, 23 April, when the streets of Stratford come alive to remember him.

The town holds special theatrical productions, literary events, processions, street entertainment and other attractions to celebrate the man born in a half-timbered house on Henley Street, who went on to be recognised as one of the greatest writers in the history of the world.

Website: www.shakespeare.org.uk/visit-the-houses/shakespeares-birthplace.html
Address: Henley Street, Stratford-upon-Avon, CV37 6QW
Nearest station: Stratford-Upon-Avon

Step into Winston Churchill's Home

Winston Churchill bought Chartwell, just outside Westerham in Kent, in 1922 and set about creating the home in which he would live until his death in 1965.

The house gives glimpses into Churchill's eccentric nature, allowing visitors to see his clothes, the study in which he wrote and dictated his books and speeches, and the studio in which he devoted time to painting. While the tiny bunk where Churchill slept is off-limits, the numerous accessible rooms help bring Britain's great wartime prime minister to life.

Website: www.nationaltrust.org.uk/chartwell/
Address: Mapleton Road, Westerham, TN16 1PS
Nearest station: Edenbridge, Sevenoaks

Explore Ebbor Gorge

A national nature reserve with steep wooded limestone ravines, Ebbor Gorge in Somerset offers a quieter alternative to the nearby Wookey Hole Caves – a major tourist attraction – with a range of interesting geological and natural features.

Three marked trails of varying lengths guide visitors through a lush green landscape of glades and limestone grassland, known for its springtime wild flowers, butterflies, insects and birdsong.

Website: www.visitsomerset.co.uk
Address: Upper Milton, Nr Wookey Hole, Wells, Somerset, BA5 3AH
Nearest station: Highbridge & Burnham

Drink at the Bell Inn

A beautiful pub that traces its origins back to the fourteenth century, the Bell Inn in Aldworth, Berkshire, is a fine example of how a village pub can still be right at the heart of a community.

A busy local, tucked away beneath the ancient Ridgeway track, The Bell Inn has been in the same family for some 250 years and warrants a listing in the *National Inventory of Historic Pub Interiors*.

Website: The Bell Inn
Address: Aldworth, Berkshire, RG8 9SE
Nearest station: Goring & Streatley

Visit the Stanley Spencer Gallery

First opened in 1962 in a former Methodist chapel in the village of Cookham, Berkshire, the Stanley Spencer Gallery collects together works of art by the celebrated English painter and Cookham resident Sir Stanley Spencer.

There can be no more fitting place to view the work of an artist so closely associated with the village of Cookham than the chapel in which he once worshipped as a member of the congregation. Many of the works on show feature the village (one of his most noted works being 'The Resurrection, Cookham'), which was a key theme of the artist's work, and where he could often be seen wandering the lanes pushing a pram in which he carried his materials.

Website: www.stanleyspencer.org.uk
Address: Stanley Spencer Gallery, High Street, Cookham SL6 9SJ
Nearest station: Cookham

STEP INSIDE EUROPE'S LARGEST TREEHOUSE

Perched in the canopy of sixteen mature lime trees in the garden of Alnwick Castle in Northumberland, and connected by rope bridges and wooden walkways, the Treehouse is a considerable improvement on those of your childhood. Opened in 2005, it was constructed at a cost of £3.3 million.

A visit also affords the opportunity to dine by a roaring fire in the Treehouse Restaurant, which specialises in locally sourced seafood, or to enjoy a cocktail in the Potting Shed bar, all while sitting in the treetops up to sixty feet off the ground.

Website: www.alnwickgarden.com/explore/whats-here/the-treehouse
Address: The Treehouse, The Alnwick Garden Denwick Lane, Alnwick, Northumberland NE66 1YU
Nearest station: Alnmouth

Watch the Grand National

The Grand National has been officially run at Aintree Racecourse in Merseyside each year since 1839, though some suggest it dates from 1836, when The Duke, a local racehorse ridden by Captain Martin Becher, won the first Great Liverpool Steeplechase.

Today, after more than 160 races, it is a major fixture in the English calendar, with a field of up to forty runners racing the four miles and four furlongs, jumping thirty fences, and competing for one of the biggest prizes in the racing year.

Website: www.aintree.co.uk/pages/grand-national/
Address: Aintree Racecourse, Ormskirk Road, Aintree, Liverpool, L9 5AS
Nearest station: Aintree

Visit Madron Holy Well

North of Penzance, at the end of a winding muddy path, lies the Madron Holy Well, thought to date from the pre-Christian period. The well is easy to find, with both signposts and traditional 'clouties', pieces of rag often tied to trees at healing wells.

Nearby, a ruined chapel from the twelfth century contains a well with running water. Many believe there has been a simple building here since the Celtic period, when the water was thought to have healing properties, attracting bathers from near and far. Local folklore tells of John Trelill, who had been a cripple for sixteen years, being cured by the water in the seventeenth century.

Website: www.cornwalls.co.uk/history/sites/madron_well.htm
Address: Bone Valley, between Heamoor and Newmill
Nearest station: Penzance

Find Peace at Greenham Common

Greenham Common was a sleepy area of the Berkshire countryside, popular for picnics, until the 1940s when it became an RAF airbase with the longest runway in Europe. It became immortalised as home of the Women's Peace Camp, when in the 1980s, 70,000 protesters took a stand against the presence of British and American nuclear weapons there.

It was reopened to the public in 2000 as common land. It is now noted for its rare and fragile ancient heathland, woodland, plants, animals and ground-nesting birds.

Website: www.greenham-common.org.uk
Address: Greenham, Newbury, Berkshire
Nearest station: Newbury

Stay at the Scarlet Hotel

Known for the sea views from each of its thirty-seven rooms, the Scarlet eco-hotel in Mawgan Porth, Cornwall, is a sustainably designed retreat with an in-house Ayurvedic spa, a cliff-top outdoor swimming pool and log-fired hot tubs with views out to sea.

As well as being a self-contained relaxing retreat for adults, the hotel also has a range of local partners who can organise invigorating off-site activities, such as surfing, deep-sea fishing and beach horse riding.

Website: www.scarlethotel.co.uk
Address: Tredragon Rd, Mawgan Porth, Cornwall TR8 4DQ
Nearest station: Bodmin Parkway

Go Letterboxing on Dartmoor

Hidden across Dartmoor are a range of small waterproof 'letterboxes', some concealed in holes or under vegetation and others easier to find. Each box contains a rubber stamp and a visitors' book, both of them important pieces of treasure for the 'letterboxers' who set out to find them armed with clues in printed leaflets or passed on by word of mouth.

The game began in 1854 when James Perrott of Chagford placed the first letterbox at Cranmere Pool on North Dartmoor, with a jar for walkers to leave their visiting cards, and since then it has grown and grown. A full catalogue of letterboxes is available from the Dartmoor Letterboxing Club and more information can be found at the Dartmoor National Park Authority visitors' centres.

Website: www.dartmoor-npa.gov.uk
Address: Dartmoor National Park Authority, Newton Abbot, Devon TQ13 9JQ
Nearest station: Newton Abbot

Walk in the Footsteps of Pilgrims

When the pilgrims of Geoffrey Chaucer's *Canterbury Tales* gathered at the Tabard Inn near London Bridge in April 1387, it was to take part in walking a well-trodden pilgrimage route to Canterbury along Watling Street, an ancient route to Dover. Although much of the original route is now the A2, it is still possible to walk quieter routes following in the footsteps of medieval pilgrims, via the trackways of the North Downs Way and the Pilgrims' Way.

The route of the Pilgrims' Way is so ancient that it links Canterbury to the pre-Norman capital of England at Winchester. Both routes skim inside the London Orbital between Mertsham and Sevenoaks, allowing modern pilgrims the chance to walk the periphery of Greater London to Canterbury.

Website: www.ldwa.org.uk/ldp/members/show_path.php?path_name=Pilgrim's+Way
Address: From Winchester to Canterbury
Nearest station: Winchester

Admire the View from Hawker's Hut

The smallest property in the ownership of the National Trust, Hawker's Hut is found near the village of Morwenstow in Cornwall. It provided a place of escape mid-19th-century for its architect, Reverend Robert Stephen Hawker, an Oxford-educated poet who was the vicar of Morwenstow.

When Hawker came to Morwenstow, the village had not had a vicar for a considerable time, and it was known to be a hotbed for smugglers and shipwrecks. Hawker built his cliff-side hut as a retreat in which to write poetry and smoke opium, using wood from the 1843 wrecks of the *Phoenix* and the *Alonzo*. Hawker's literary friends Alfred Tennyson and Charles Kingsley are both known to have visited during their time in Cornwall.

Website: www.themagicofcornwall.com/blog/?p=1385
Address: Morwenstow, near Bude, North Cornwall
Nearest station: Barnstaple, Bodmin

Tresspass on Kinder Scout

In April 1932, more than 400 people strode out onto the bleak moors of Kinder Scout in the Peak District, in an act of mass trespass designed to provoke a debate about access for members of the public to areas of open countryside.

Though five people were arrested and some even received prison sentences, the trespass – organised by the British Workers Sports Federation – was successful in raising awareness about access, and later in 1932, 10,000 walkers assembled for a rally in the Winnats Pass near Castleton. The action is credited with inspiring 1949 legislation establishing our much-loved National Parks. A number of trails leave Hayfield, from where the original trespassers set off, so you can retrace their routes.

Website: www.peakdistrictinformation.com/features/kinder.php
Address: Kinder Scout, National Nature Reserve, Dark Peak, Derbyshire
Nearest station: Edale

RENT YOUR OWN CASTLE

Completed in 1502 to protect the entrance to Dartmouth Harbour in Devon, Kingswear Castle worked with Dartmouth Castle on the other side of the river to defend the town against attacks by pirates and foreign ships. After falling into disrepair, the Castle found a new life as a summer residence of wealthy bachelor Charles Seale-Hayne in 1855, saving it from potential ruin.

Except for a brief period of use during the Second World War – when it once again became a military outpost – the Castle remained a private home until 1987, when the Landmark Trust charity acquired it and began allowing visitors to rent it for holidays. It still makes a fine spot for a break, and visitors can enjoy watching the waves crashing on the rocks below from beside a roaring fire.

Website: www.landmarktrust.org.uk/search-and-book/properties/kingswear-castle-8737
Address: Kingswear Castle, Near Dartmouth, Devon
Nearest station: Totnes

Walk on Clevedon Pier

Originally built in the 1860s, Clevedon Pier in the small North Somerset town of Clevedon is the only Grade I-listed pier open to the public, as well as being among the earliest Victorian piers still in existence. It was designed to allow paddle steamers to dock for services to South Wales and further afield.

Even after the building of the Severn Railway Tunnel to South Wales, the pier continued as a docking station for pleasure boats, and recent years have seen a reprisal of this service, taking passengers from Clevedon to destinations such as the islands of Flat Holm and Steep Holm. Despite a collapse of two elements of the pier in 1970, a local campaign saved the structure from demolition and it finally reopened in 1998.

Website: www.clevedonpier.com
Address: The Toll House, Clevedon BS21 7QU
Nearest station: Yatton

See England's Oldest Mosque

The Shah Jahan Mosque in Woking, Surrey, was Britain's first purpose-built mosque, built by Hungarian-born Orientalist Dr Gottlieb Wilhelm Leitner and completed in 1889. More than a century later, the mosque is a vibrant centre of the local Muslim community, and welcomes visitors.

Educated at King's College London, Leitner spent time in British India before returning to England in 1883 to establish the Oriental Institute in Woking, where he subsequently built the mosque as a result of a donation from the Begum Shah Jahan, the ruler of Bhopal.

Website: www.shahjahanmosque.org.uk
Address: 149 Oriental Rd, Woking GU22 7BA
Nearest station: Woking

Search for Primroses at Hughenden Manor

From the late nineteenth century onwards, 19 April has been celebrated as Primrose Day in England, marking the anniversary of the death of Prime Minister Benjamin Disraeli, whose favourite flower was the primrose.

When Disraeli died in 1881, Queen Victoria sent a wreath of primroses – which flower in April – for his funeral. The flowers can be found in the gardens and surrounding woodland at Hughenden Manor, near High Wycombe in Buckinghamshire, which was Disraeli's grand home from 1848 until his death.

Website: www.nationaltrust.org.uk/hughenden/
Address: Hughenden Manor, High Wycombe, Bucks. HP14 4LA
Nearest station: High Wycombe

Ride the World's First Passenger Railway

A regular exhibit at Manchester's Museum of Science and Industry allows visitors to take a ride on the very site where the first passenger steam trains once travelled, on what was the Liverpool and Manchester Railway.

The museum occupies the buildings of Liverpool Road Station, the oldest surviving passenger railway station in the world, and on some days visitors even get to ride behind Planet, a replica of an 1830 Robert Stephenson and Company steam locomotive. The short journey also runs alongside Granada Studios, allowing passengers to peer into the site where TV classics such as *Coronation Street* are filmed.

Website: www.mosi.org.uk
Address: Liverpool Rd, Manchester M3 4FP
Nearest station: Manchester Piccadilly

Spot Puffins at Bempton Cliffs

During the breeding season, the 400-foot-high cliffs at Bempton on the North Yorkshire coast are the best place in England to see Atlantic Puffins, which arrive in April to lay eggs in crevices in the rock face. The RSPB has a visitor centre at the cliffs, from where nature trails run to the best viewing spots.

Thousands of puffins return to the cliffs each year to breed, in a season that continues until July, with adult birds regularly visiting their young with small fish, until they grow large enough to fly the nest. The cliffs are also home to the largest mainland gannet colony in Britain, and the spring is a good time to spot breeding gannets.

Website: www.rspb.org.uk/reserves/guide/b/bemptoncliffs
Address: Visitor Centre, Cliff Ln, Bempton, Bridlington,
East Riding of Yorkshire YO15 1JF
Nearest station: Bempton

FIND THE SOURCE OF THE THAMES

Though many are happy with the received wisdom that the source of the Thames is at Thames Head, marked by a monument a short walk across a field from the village of Kemble in the Gloucestershire countryside, others maintain that the real source is at Seven Springs, ten miles away, where a Thames tributary, the River Churn, rises near Cheltenham.

The Environment Agency and Ordnance Survey also have their own ideas, listing the source as Trewsbury Mead, a short walk from Thames Head. Whatever the truth, it is hard to believe that a river that ultimately becomes one of the most important in the world begins in this tranquil stretch of English countryside.

Website: www.visitthames.co.uk/about-the-river
Address: Kemble, Cirencester
Nearest station: Kemble

Explore the Whipsnade Tree Cathedral

In 1930, following a visit to the new Anglican Cathedral in Liverpool, Edmond Blyth began to plant the Tree Cathedral on land at Chapel Farm in Whipsnade, Bedfordshire, as a tribute to contemporaries who had not returned from fighting in the First World War, in which he had lost a number of friends.

Though completion of the project was delayed by the Second World War, it was finally achieved in the 1950s, and Blyth continued to manage it until his death in 1969. His son, Tom, took over its care until his own death in 1978, since when the Tree Cathedral has been in the care of the National Trust, who continue to open it to the public, supported by the Whipsnade Tree Cathedral Fund.

Website: www.nationaltrust.org.uk/whipsnade-tree-cathedral
Address: Yew Tree Cottage, 33 Pebblemoor, Edlesborough LU6 2LL
Nearest station: Bedford

Collect Sea Glass on Seaham Beach

The beach at Seaham in County Durham is famous among beachcombers for its 'end of day' sea glass – beautiful pieces of coloured glass that can be found among the shingle and sand – originating in the bottleworks of Victorian entrepreneur John Candlish, who had six glasshouses in the town.

In a time of less stringent environmental regulation, the glass factories would pour any waste glass into the sea at the end of each day, leaving it to be smoothed by the motion of the waves, eventually producing stunning little pieces of glass that can still be found today.

Address: Seaham seafront
Nearest station: Seaham

THINGS TO DO TODAY:

May

By May, summer has arrived in England's far South, and is slowly starting to spread through the rest of the country, welcomed by festivals that start on May Day. This can still be a month of contrasts: as garden flowers bloom in the Kentish countryside, frosts are not unheard of, especially in Cumbria and Northumberland.

As the gardens of country homes reopen for the summer season, flattened seas also offer easy passage to the offshore islands such as Lundy, the Farne Islands and the Isles of Scilly, where seals sun themselves in crisp sunshine and puffins and other sea birds arrive for summer breeding. At sea, the first basking sharks arrive off the coasts, as fishermen chase haddock and herring and the spring lobster season begins.

Attend the Padstow 'Obby 'Oss Festival

First recorded in 1803, and thought to date back much further, Padstow's 'Obby 'Oss Festival is a traditional English May Day event that sees thousands throng the streets of the small Cornish town for a day of celebration, to embrace the changing of the seasons through song and dance.

The centre of the celebrations are the 'Obby 'Osses (hobby horses), which emerge from their long winter slumber to dance in the streets with traditional dancers, accompanied by the sounds of drums and accordions. The celebrations begin at the Golden Lion Inn around midnight, and go on throughout the day, focussed around the town maypole.

Website: www.padstow.com/obby_oss/obby_oss.php
Address: Red Brick Building, North Quay, Padstow PL28 8AF
Nearest station: Bodmin

Follow the Hastings Jack-in-the-Green

A modern revival of a tradition familiar to the people of Victorian Hastings, the Jack-in-the-Green takes place in the Sussex town in early May, with a whole weekend of music, dance, performance and colour in a celebration based on the end-of-season festivities of chimney sweeps.

The festival culminates with a Monday parade through the narrow streets of Hastings Old Town to the hilltop ruins of Hastings Castle, with Morris dancing, bands and a star turn by the 'Jack-in-the-Green', a garlanded figure who is symbolically torn apart in a ceremony to release the spirit of summer.

Website: www.hastingsjack.co.uk
Address: Locations throughout Hastings
Nearest station: Hastings

Wander in Hundred Acre Wood

A A Milne based the fictional home of Winnie-the-Pooh on a real place close to his home at Cotchford Farm in East Sussex, with Hundred Acre Wood inspired by the real Five Hundred Acre Wood, a dense stretch of the ancient Ashdown Forest.

Walks from Gills Lap car park on the B2026 – the inspiration for Galleons Lap in the books – take in such sights as the North Pole ('DICSovERED By PooH'), the Heffalump Trap and Eeyore's Gloomy Place, and also pass a memorial to A A Milne and E H Shepard, who illustrated the books.

Website: www.pooh-corner.org/map.shtml
Address: Ashdown Forest and Cotchford Farm, Hartfield, East Sussex
Nearest station: East Grinstead

Dance the Furry Dance

An ancient dance custom, the origins of which are uncertain, grips the residents of Helston in Cornwall on 8 May each year, as couples dance through the streets to the music of the Helston Town Band. The town is decorated with flags, flowers and greenery, and everyone wears lily of the valley in their buttonholes. Spectators turn out in droves to watch the celebrations and listen to music played from memory by the town's musicians.

The dancing is held in four stages, beginning in the early morning, at 7 a.m., with ladies in summer dresses, and men in grey flannels and white shirts. The children get their turn mid-morning, dressed all in white, and the midday dance – traditionally for the higher classes – sees ladies dance in full-length gowns with their menfolk in morning suits and tails. For the early evening dance, attire returns to a more relaxed style.

Website: www.helston-online.co.uk
Address: Various locations throughout Helston
Nearest station: Camborne

Watch a Show Above the Waves at the Minack Theatre

One of the world's most atmospheric theatres, the Minack sits on the cliffs above Porthcurno in Cornwall, and hosts open-air performances on a rocky outcrop above the crashing waves.

The brainchild of Rowena Cade, who offered her garden to local thespians for a performance of *The Tempest*, the theatre has held summer performances since the 1930s, when it was built by Cade with the help of her gardener, Billy Rawlings, and his mate, Charles Thomas Angove.

Website: www.minack.com
Address: Minack Theatre, Porthcurno, Penzance, Cornwall TR19 6JU
Nearest station: Penzance

Visit the Home of *The Compleat Angler*

In 1653, Izaak Walton published *The Compleat Angler*, a book that has become one of the most loved and reprinted books in the English language. Two years later, in May 1655, Walton bought a cottage beside Meece Brook in the tiny hamlet of Shallowford, a property he retained until his death.

The cottage passed to the people of Stafford in Walton's will, and today it contains a small angling museum, telling the story of Walton and his work. Surrounded by neat gardens of herbs and roses, it is open to the public during the summer months.

Website: www.staffordbc.gov.uk/izaak-waltons-cottage
Address: Izaak Walton's Cottage, Worston Ln, Shallowford ST16 0PA
Nearest station: Stone (Staffs.)

Rejoice with the Rochester Sweeps

A long weekend of partying in the shadow of Rochester Castle, the Rochester Sweeps Festival is another revival of the age-old May Day tradition once held by chimney sweeps to mark the end of their season.

The festival, which was revived by local historian Gordon Newton in 1981, takes place throughout Rochester, attracting Morris sides and folk musicians from around the country to come and welcome the summer.

Address: Rochester Castle Gardens, Castle Hill, Rochester ME1 1SW
Nearest station: Rochester

Climb Skiddaw

Towering 3,053 feet above the town of Keswick in the Lake District, Skiddaw is the sixth-highest mountain in England. A path to the summit rises steeply from the car park at Latrigg, meaning walkers need strong legs to haul themselves upwards over a smaller peak called Little Man.

The peak is made largely of scree and offers fantastic views, and there is a choice of paths for returning to the base of the mountain.

Address: Keswick, the Lake District
Nearest station: Penrith

Go Punting in Cambridge

A traditional part of Cambridge University student life, punts are available along the River Cam, with one of the most popular spots being the stretch beside the late-Gothic King's College, whose beautiful chapel offers one of the city's most iconic views.

It's an excellent way to relax for an hour or so, especially with a picnic basket or a glass of wine, and punts are available to operate yourself or with a chauffeur, should you doubt your steering skills.

Website: www.scudamores.com
Address: Granta Place, Mill Lane, Cambridge, CB2 1RS
Nearest station: Cambridge

MEET THE CERNE ABBAS GIANT

Known for his 'interesting' appearance, the Cerne Abbas Giant is a huge chalk outline of a naked man, carved into the chalk bedrock of the Dorset hills. Though the earliest written reference to the Giant dates from the eighteenth century, his origin is unknown, and some believe he is much older, possibly connected to the Iron Age earthworks found nearby.

Perhaps as a result of his physique, a visit to the Giant is said to increase fertility, and childless couples are known to visit while attempting to conceive. Indeed, it is said that spending the night at the Giant in early May has the power to boost fertility, as a result of proximity to a certain part of his anatomy.

Website: www.nationaltrust.org.uk/cerne-giant/
Address: Cerne Abbas, DT2 7AL
Nearest station: Maiden Newton

Admire the View from Selsley Common

An area of common land overlooking the town of Stroud in Gloucestershire, Selsley Common comprises nearly 160 acres of limestone grassland with stunning views over the Severn Vale and towards the Stroud Valleys, which once boasted around 150 woollen mills creating cloth for export around the world.

Now popular with paragliders, Selsley is said to have been used as a camp and lookout by soldiers loyal to Prince Edward – who was later to become King Edward I – during the Second Baron's War of 1263–67. It also boasts a Neolithic long barrow called The Toots. Beneath the common, Selsley Church, designed by G F Bodley, is celebrated for its gallery of Pre-Raphaelite stained glass by William Morris and others.

Website: www.escapetothecotswolds.org.uk
Address: Selsley Common, near Stroud
Nearest station: Stroud

Take a Trip to the Farne Islands

Boats leave the village of Seahouses, on the Northumberland coast, daily from May to September for day trips to the Farne Islands, a haven for seals and sea birds such as puffins, guillemots, razorbills and terns. The breeding season begins in May and an occasional stop-off on Staple Island can be arranged, to observe tens of thousands of seabirds packing the cliffs.

It is occasionally also possible to land on Inner Farne, the largest of the islands, famous for its association with St Cuthbert, who spent time here between becoming Bishop of Lindisfarne in 684 and dying on the island in 687.

Website: www.nationaltrust.org.uk/farne-islands/
Address: Near Seahouses, off the Northumberland Coast
Nearest station: Chathill

Visit Sutton Hoo

In May 1939, self-taught Suffolk archaeologist Basil Brown began to excavate a mound at Sutton Hoo in Suffolk, under the watchful eye of landowner Edith Pretty. Though the treasures found in a ship burial here are now held by the British Museum, the 255-acre site beside the River Deben in Suffolk is still open to the public.

The estate is managed by the National Trust and its fields of grassy mounds are home to cemeteries from the sixth and seventh centuries, inside one of which was the undisturbed seventh-century ship burial that gave up the famous treasures.

Website: www.nationaltrust.org.uk/sutton-hoo/
Address: Tranmer House, Woodbridge, IP12 3DJ
Nearest station: Woodbridge

Attend the Holmfirth Festival of Folk

An annual free festival in Yorkshire's Holme Valley, the Holmfirth Festival of Folk brings folk music and dance from around the country to the streets of Holmfirth, with large crowds of all ages coming out to support the event.

The festival takes place in the town's streets and pubs over a weekend in mid-May, and also offers folk workshops, dance recitals and family events, with the Saturday night ceilidh usually a highlight.

Website: http://holmfirthfestivaloffolk.co.uk
Address: Various locations in Holmfirth
Nearest station: Brockholes

Visit the Gordon Boswell Romany Museum

A unique museum on the outskirts of Spalding in Lincolnshire, the Gordon Boswell Romany Museum is a labour of love for Mr Boswell, who has amassed a huge collection of photographs and artefacts covering 150 years of Romany life.

The museum contains a fortune-telling tent and Romany wagons, and even offers the opportunity for small groups to enjoy a day out in a horse-drawn Gypsy Vardo, complete with a steak meal cooked over a traditional stick fire in the depths of the Lincolnshire countryside.

Website: www.boswell-romany-museum.com
Address: Clay Lake, Spalding PE12 6BL
Nearest station: Spalding

See the Bowthorpe Oak

Thought to be more than 1,000 years old, Lincolnshire's Bowthorpe Oak stands in a grassy meadow behind Bowthorpe Park Farm near Manthorpe, and visitors can see it for a small charge that is donated to charity.

The tree has an interesting history, and legend has it that previous residents of the farm used the hollow interior to host parties boasting more than thirty guests, whilst an eighteenth-century nobleman is said to have entertained twenty people at a sit-down dinner inside. Today, the tree lives a much more sedate existence, still growing strongly despite its hollow trunk.

Website: www.wildaboutbritain.co.uk
Address: Bowthorpe Park Farm, Manthorpe, Bourne, Lincolnshire
Nearest station: Grantham

Explore the Studios of Oxfordshire Artists

Established in 1981, the annual Oxfordshire Artweeks are a three-week open-studio event for Oxfordshire artists, allowing members of the public to see special exhibitions in the spaces in which artists create their works.

The festival takes place each May and venues are found throughout the towns and villages of Oxfordshire, with events in certain areas in each week, offering art-lovers an opportunity to meet local artists and talk about their work.

Website: www.artweeks.org
Address: Across the towns and villages of Oxfordshire
Nearest station: Oxford

Take a Boat Trip from Lulworth Cove

A stunning limestone horseshoe bay formed around 10,000 years ago, Lulworth Cove continues to be slowly eroded by the sea, although its serene pebble beach and the many boats seeking shelter from the rougher seas outside create an air of calm that suggests otherwise.

Beyond the bay is a spectacular rugged coastline, which can be viewed by taking one of the frequent boat trips that run from the beach.

Website: www.lulworthonline.co.uk
Address: Lulworth Cove, West Lulworth
Nearest station: Wool

Ride the Cornish Sleeper

One of only two sleeper services on the British railway network, the Night Riviera Sleeper provides passengers with a bed for the night so that they can go to sleep at London Paddington and wake up in Penzance. The service runs six nights a week, with one- and two-bed compartments linking London to a number of destinations in Somerset, Devon and Cornwall, finally arriving in Penzance at around 8 o'clock.

A sleeper train has been running on the Great Western route since 1877, when the first sleeper car was introduced on the Plymouth-to-London line. For those who don't fancy an early night, the service also boasts a lounge car with a range of wine, beer, spirits, soft drinks and snacks.

Website: www.firstgreatwestern.co.uk
Address: Runs between London Paddington and Penzance, Cornwall
Nearest station: London Paddington, Penzance

See the Maunsell Forts

Designed by Guy Maunsell to defend London during the Second World War, the Maunsell Forts in the Thames Estuary were once home to full military garrisons and anti-aircraft guns, charged with shooting down the planes of the Luftwaffe before they reached their destination.

No longer needed in the post-war period, the Forts were decommissioned in the 1950s but remained in place. Pirate radio stations subsequently occupied some of the forts, and another — HM Fort Roughs — was taken over by Major Paddy Roy Bates, who declared it the independent Principality of Sealand in 1975. Today, the forts are uninhabited and can be seen from boats, which take visitors on occasional trips from the North Kent coast.

Website: www.undergroundkent.co.uk/maunsell_towers.htm
Address: Herne Bay, Kent
Nearest station: Herne Bay

WALK TO THE EDGE OF THE SOLAR SYSTEM

The Kent village of Otford, near Sevenoaks, is the centre of what might be the world's largest scale model. Based around the village playing field, the model solar system has the Sun represented by a dome 303 millimetres in diameter and the planets by engravings on flat discs, all spaced to scale and representing the planets' positions on 1 January 2000.

The model extends far beyond the boundaries of the village, with the nearest star, Proxima Centauri, at the Griffith Observatory in Los Angeles and Barnard's Star displayed at Stanley Museum in the Falkland Islands. The model was designed by local man David Thomas, who helped to maintain and promote it until his death in 2010.

Website: www.solarsystem.otford.info/
Address: Otford Parish Council and Heritage Centre, 21 High Street, Otford, Kent TN14 5PG
Nearest station: Otford

See the Tulips of Spalding

The region around Spalding in Lincolnshire is one of England's most important flower-growing areas, particularly known for its tulips. Every year, the new crop of blooms is celebrated in the town centre with the Spalding Flower Parade, a tradition dating from the 1950s.

The parade sees huge floats decorated with up to 100,000 tulip heads pass through the town, accompanied by marching bands and representatives of community organisations. Outside the town, acres of fields offer a display of tulip colour, making it a pleasant spot for a springtime cycle.

Website: www.spalding-flower-parade.org.uk
Address: Locations across Spalding
Nearest station: Spalding

Celebrate Oak Apple Day in Castleton

Since 1660, Oak Apple Day, or Royal Oak Day, on 29 May has been celebrated to commemorate the restoration of the English monarchy. Castleton in Derbyshire marks the occasion with the most vigour.

The celebrations revolve around a Garland King and Queen, who parade around the local pubs on horseback wearing seventeenth-century dress, with the King completely covered in a huge garland of wild flowers. At the end of the parade, the heavy garland is raised to the top of St Edmund's Church tower, while the smaller wreath of the Queen is placed on the war memorial, and then the village celebrates into the evening with plenty of singing and dancing.

Website: www.castleton.co.uk
Address: Various locations in Castleton
Nearest station: Edale

Chase the Cooper's Hill Cheese

Locals have been chasing a circular Double Gloucester cheese down a terrifyingly steep slope on the edge of the Cotswolds near Brockworth, Gloucester, since at least the early nineteenth century, in a tradition said to be connected to the maintenance of commoners' grazing rights in the area.

Despite attempts to end the rolling due to health-and-safety concerns, up to 5,000 spectators still come to perch on the hillside and watch competitors hurl themselves down the hill for the chance to win glory, a cheese and a place in the Gloucestershire history books.

Website: www.cheese-rolling.co.uk/index1.htm
Address: Cooper's Hill, Brockworth
Nearest station: Ashchurch for Tewkesbury

STAY ON A PIRATE ISLAND

Once visited by Celts and Vikings, Lundy Island in the Bristol Channel was, by the thirteenth century, the base of the Marisco family. William de Marisco, implicated in a plot to murder Henry III, retreated to the island to live as a pirate until he was eventually captured.

In the seventeenth century, the island was seized and held by the Moroccan Barbary Pirates for five years, and in 1610 it became a base for Thomas Salkeld, who tried and failed to have himself crowned 'Pirate King of Lundy'. Today, Lundy is in the care of the Landmark Trust as a destination for day trips and holidays, and even has its own pub, the Marisco Tavern.

Website: www.lundyisland.co.uk/
Address: Lundy Shore Office, The Quay, Bideford, Devon, EX39 2LY
Nearest station: Barnstaple

Attend the Cambridge Beer Festival

England's longest-running beer festival has been held in Cambridge since 1974, moving in 2001 to a marquee on Jesus Green, where it is still held at the end of May.

Popular with locals and students from the city's universities, the festival offers more than 200 different ales and has been known to attract more than 30,000 people over its annual run.

Website: www.cambridgebeerfestival.com
Address: Jesus Green, Cambridge
Nearest station: Cambridge

Sail on a Thames Barge

Topsail Charters was established in the late 1980s, by Stephanie Valentine and Paul Jeffries, with a plan to preserve Thames barges by putting them back into use, and by 2006, around 11,000 people a year were taking up their invitation to enjoy a trip on their boats.

The company operates five barges, including grain barge *Kitty*, built by Cann of Harwich in 1895, *Cabby*, the last wooden sailing barge ever built (in 1928), and *Hydrogen*, the largest surviving wooden barge. Their trips take passengers around East Anglia and the Thames Estuary for birdwatching, sightseeing and lunches.

Website: www.top-sail.co.uk
Address: Various locations, including Ipswich and Maldon
Nearest station: Witham

Welcome the Summer at Bampton

The bank holiday weekend in late May is an active time in the Oxfordshire village of Bampton, with the annual Shirt Race (raced in nightshirts) held on the Saturday, and the village's traditional Morris dancers taking to the streets on Monday.

Organised by the Society for the Preservation of Ancient Junketing, the Shirt Race sees competitors pushed in prams undertake a circuit of the village, downing drinks. On the Monday, Bampton Morris welcomes the summer with a traditional fertility cake and dancing in the village.

Website: www.bamptonoxon.co.uk
Address: Various locations in Bampton, West Oxfordshire
Nearest station: Oxford

Watch the Tetbury Woolsack Race

The market town of Tetbury in Gloucestershire has celebrated its connection to the wool trade with a Woolsack Race in late May for more than thirty years.

The town sits on the ancient drovers' road between Bristol and Oxford, which was once a well-trodden route for drovers and their flocks, and today, men and women carry woolsacks, custom-made by the British Wool Federation, between local pubs in honour of their forefathers.

Website: www.tetburywoolsack.co.uk
Address: Tetbury town centre and Gumstool Hill
Nearest station: Kemble

See Brighton's Royal Pavilion

The grand seaside retreat of George, Prince of Wales, who later became Prince Regent and then George IV, was originally rented as a modest farmhouse, chosen for its seaside climate and access to sea-water treatments, which were fashionable at the time.

By the time of George IV's death in 1830, the holiday home had been completely transformed into an Indian-style palace, designed by John Nash and featuring the grand central dome, minarets, pinnacles and chimney-stacks we still see today. When Queen Victoria came to the throne in 1837, however, she decided not to use the Pavilion and so it was sold to the people of Brighton in 1850 and remains open to the public today.

Website: www.brighton-hove-rpml.org.uk
Address: 4–5 Pavilion Buildings, Brighton, BN1 1EE
Nearest station: Brighton

Watch the Cotswold Olimpicks

Tracing their origins back to the seventeenth century, when the first event was organised by local resident Robert Dover, the Cotswold Olimpicks usually take place on the Friday of Whitsun week, in late May or early June, at Dover's Hill near Chipping Campden, in the North Cotswolds.

The event is characterised by traditional sports such as shin-kicking, tug-of-war, a 'champion of the hill' race and the Olimpick five-mile race, but also features marching bands, Morris dancing, a bonfire, torchlight display and fireworks, continuing until midnight with further entertainment in town.

Website: www.olimpickgames.co.uk
Address: Kingcomb Lane, Chipping Campden
Nearest station: Moreton-in-Marsh

June

June is marked by abundance, with long days bringing people outdoors to enjoy blooming gardens and fresh green lawns. The month was called 'Tri-Milchi' by the Anglo-Saxons, as the lush grass allowed cows to be milked three times a day. Today, the month sees rich meadows filled with wild flowers and the start of the fruit-and-vegetable season. The Strawbery Moon (June's full moon) heralds the first strawberries of the season.

Midsummer brings the strongest sun of the year, and England is at its liveliest, with quintessentially English events: tennis at Wimbledon, opera at Glyndebourne and the world's best music festival at Glastonbury. Many celebrate the summer solstice, notably in the South West at ancient sites such as Avebury and Stonehenge.

Climb Glastonbury Tor

Rising above the town like a pyramid, and topped off by a mysterious church tower, it is not hard to see why Glastonbury Tor so easily captures the imagination. The Tor is thought to be the peak of the ancient Isle of Avalon, and was once an island itself, rising from the marshy Somerset Levels.

Legend has it that the island was visited by King Arthur, Saint Patrick and even Jesus Christ's tin-trading uncle, Joseph of Arimathea. The monks at Glastonbury Abbey even questioned whether a young Jesus himself had visited, in a story immortalised in the popular hymn 'Jerusalem'.

Website: www.nationaltrust.org.uk/glastonbury-tor/
Address: Glastonbury, Somerset
Nearest station: Castle Cary

Take a Boat to Warkworth Hermitage

A short distance from the Northumberland town of Warkworth, the hermitage is tucked away in a serene spot near the river and accessible only by boat. It was built by the Percy family of Warkworth Castle and was home to a resident priest between the fourteenth and sixteenth centuries.

During the summer months, an oarsman is often on hand to row visitors up the River Coquet to view the hermitage. The main chapel and smaller chamber were carved directly out of the rock, and much of the carving is still visible today, along with the original stone constructions outside.

Website: www.english-heritage.org.uk
Address: Castle Terrace, Warkworth, Northumberland, NE65 0UJ
Nearest station: Alnmouth

Walk Hadrian's Wall

Walking along the Hadrian's Wall National Trail in June can be particularly rewarding for those with a sturdy pair of boots looking for stunning vistas. Running across eighty-four miles of rugged moorland, green fields and industrial landscapes, the walk follows the length of the wall.

Much of the route is unchanged since Roman times, and eight excavated forts dot the path, helping visitors to get a sense of what life might have been like for Roman soldiers, posted to the edge of the known world by a distant empire, and staring off into the abyss against attacks from those considered to be marauding savages.

Website: www.visithadrianswall.co.uk/
Address: Lanercost Tea Room, Lanercost, Cumbria, CA8 2HQ
Nearest station: Newcastle (Central); Prudhoe; Stocksfield; Wylam

Visit the Birthplace of Edward Elgar

Found in the village of Lower Broadheath, just a few miles outside Worcester, the Elgar Birthplace Museum celebrates the life and work of the composer Sir Edward Elgar, and offers a unique opportunity to see inside the cottage where he was born.

Elgar was born in the cottage on 2 June 1857, the fourth of seven children and the first to be born in the house, which now boasts a neighbouring visitors' centre showcasing a wide range of objects relating to his life.

Website: www.elgarmuseum.org/
Address: Crown East Lane, Lower Broadheath, Worcester WR2 6RH
Nearest station: Worcester Foregate Street; Worcester Shrub Hill

EAT NETTLES AT THE BOTTLE INN

The World Stinging Nettle Eating Challenge grew out of an argument in the 1980s between two farmers over who had the longest nettles on his land. One of them was supposedly so sure that his nettles were the longest that he said if anyone could beat it, he would eat it – and when someone stepped forward with a longer nettle, he did.

The challenge was born, and although the competition occasionally moves date, it is always held at the Bottle Inn, a sixteenth-century Dorset pub. Competitors strip the nettle leaves from their stalks and eat them. After an hour, the lengths of stalk are assessed and the winner is the person with the greatest accumulated stalk length.

Website: www.nettleeating.co.uk/
Address: The Bottle Inn, Marshwood, Bridport, DT6 5QJ
Nearest station: Maiden Newton

Relax Beneath the Palms of Tresco Abbey Gardens

The subtropical climate of Tresco, the second-biggest island of the Isles of Scilly, allows for flora and fauna that would never survive on the mainland. This is amply demonstrated at the tropical garden at Tresco Abbey, with species from eighty countries of varying climates growing in the open air.

The garden was begun by Augustus Smith, the Victorian owner of the islands, who built a home at Tresco Abbey, beside the ruins of St Nicholas Priory, and began creating a garden protected by walls from the Atlantic winds. The garden is now home to a collection of palm trees and exotic plants unlike any seen on the mainland, and also houses the Valhalla collection of nautical figureheads from the days of sail.

Website: www.tresco.co.uk/what-to-do/abbey-garden
Address: Tresco Abbey Garden, Tresco, Isles of Scilly, TR24 0QQ
Nearest station: Penzance

Take tea in the Orchard Tea Garden

One spring morning in 1897, a group of students from the nearby University of Cambridge asked Mrs Stevenson, the owner of Orchard House in Grantchester, if she would serve them tea beneath the blossoming fruit trees of her orchard instead of on the front lawn as usual. And so the Orchard Tea Garden was born.

Since then, a visit to the Grantchester Tea Rooms has become a Cambridge tradition. The poet Rupert Brooke, who lived for a while in rooms at Orchard House, wrote one of his most celebrated poems about it. Since the 1920s, students have punted along the river to Grantchester for alfresco Champagne breakfasts following their post-exam May Balls, which confusingly take place in early June.

Website: www.orchard-grantchester.com/
Address: 45-47 Mill Way, Grantchester CB3 9ND
Nearest station: Cambridge

Drink at the Woolpack, Slad

The Woolpack is a beautiful freehouse in the sleepy Slad Valley, immortalised by Laurie Lee in *Cider With Rosie*. Lee remained a regular at the pub until his death in 1997, sitting outside on summer afternoons and — legend has it — taking tourists who asked to see Laurie Lee's grave on wild-goose chases around the churchyard.

The pub traces its history back to the 1640s, when the wool industry was strong in the area, and woolpacks such as those that feature on the pub's sign were a common sight in the Slad Valley. Today, its compact interior is busy most evenings, and the bar serves ales from the local Uley and Stroud Breweries.

Website: www.thewoolpackinn-slad.com
Address: The Woolpack, Slad, Gloucestershire, GL6 7QA
Nearest station: Stroud

Have a Picnic at Castle Howard

Set in a vast landscaped park in the Howardian Hills, Castle Howard is a grand stately home designed by Sir John Vanbrugh, and probably best known as the setting for adaptations of Evelyn Waugh's *Brideshead Revisited*.

The sheer scale of the estate makes it a fine spot for a picnic, with plenty of room to lay out on well-kept lawns. For those unable to bring a picnic with them, the Howard Estate's farm shop has its own delicatessen, selling all you could ever need.

Website: www.castlehoward.co.uk
Address: Castle Howard, York YO60 7DA
Nearest station: York

Attend the Bradford Mela

Originally a small local event held in the summer of 1988, the Bradford Mela was the first event of its kind in Britain. Its aim was to recreate the festive spirit of the Indian subcontinent in a town with an already-well-established South Asian community as a result of immigration since the 1950s.

The festival has grown into a vibrant celebration of the culture of South Asia, and now attracts tens of thousands of visitors of all ages and backgrounds to experience food, drink, music and street performances across a number of stages and areas.

Website: www.bradfordmela.org.uk
Address: Peel Park, Bradford, West Yorkshire
Nearest station: Bradford

See the Chillingham Cattle

Some of the rarest animals on earth can be seen at Chillingham in Northumberland, where less than 100 Chillingham Wild Cattle – the final survivors of the wild herds that once roamed Britain's forests – are still to be found, grazing quietly.

The cattle became cut off from the rest of the world in the Middle Ages, when the parkland they grazed was enclosed. For more than 800 years, the cattle remained physically and genetically isolated from other animals. The park and the haunted castle of the same name are now open to visitors during the summer months.

Website: www.chillinghamwildcattle.com/
Address: Chillingham, Alnwick, Northumberland
Nearest station: Alnmouth

Celebrate Filly Loo

Every June on the Friday closest to midsummer, the residents of Ashmore in Dorset gather around the village pond to celebrate Filly Loo, with folk music and dancing in a revival of an age-old feast.

The celebration bears many of the hallmarks of other English folk traditions, with a Green Man who leads the first dance and an ancient night-time horn dance like the one held each September at Abbots Bromley in Staffordshire, before coming to a symbolic end, with the holding of hands around the village dew pond.

Website: www.visit-dorset.com/whats-on/ashmore-filly-loo-p383193
Address: Ashmore, Dorset by the village pond
Nearest station: Tisbury

Go to the Opera at Glyndebourne

A different type of music festival to rival Glastonbury takes place every summer at Glyndebourne in Sussex, and is probably what you'd expect from an event established in 1934 by wealthy Etonian landowner John Christie and his opera-singer wife, Audrey Mildmay. Unlike many rowdy June festivals, the annual Glyndebourne Festival is a more genteel affair, where punters are more likely to be wearing black tie than a pair of wellington boots.

Originally held in the main house at Glyndebourne, the festival moved to a purpose-built opera house – designed by Michael Hopkins – within the grounds during the 1990s. Performances include a particularly long interval, in order to allow visitors to eat their picnic dinners on one of Glyndebourne's extensive lawns before returning for the second half.

Website: http://glyndebourne.com
Address: Glyndebourne, Lewes, East Sussex, BN8 5UU
Nearest station: Lewes

Walk in Constable Country

By the summer of 1816, when he returned to paint Flatford Mill a few months before his marriage to childhood friend Maria Bicknell, John Constable had already been painting the area for many years. He had established a routine of spending the winter in London and painting in the summer around East Bergholt, the village where he was born.

Though he only sold twenty paintings in England during his lifetime, Constable is now recognised as one of the country's greatest painters. A walk from East Bergholt passes his first studio and offers the chance to stand where Constable produced some of his finest paintings: Flatford Mill, once owned by his father; Willy Lott's House, the enduring setting for *The Hay Wain*; and gazing across sleepy Dedham Vale.

Website: www.field-studies-council.org/centres/flatfordmill.aspx
Address: Flatford Mill Field Centre, East Bergholt, Suffolk, CO7 6UL
Nearest station: Manningtree

Visit the birthplace of British motorsport

When it first opened in June 1907, the 2.75-mile banked track at Brooklands in Surrey was the world's first purpose-built race track. Home to countless motor-racing records, the track hosted the world's first twenty-four-hour motoring event within eleven days of opening, and was the venue for the first British Grand Prix, in 1926.

Brooklands also became a centre for aviation, and by 1918 it was Britain's largest aircraft manufacturing centre. At the start of the Second World War in 1939, motor racing ceased as the site prioritised the production of aircraft, an industry that continued here until 1987. Today, the Brooklands Museum tells the stories of motor racing and aviation at Brooklands, and it is still possible to see sections of the steeply banked track.

Website: www.brooklandsmuseum.com
Address: Brooklands Museum, Brooklands Road, Weybridge KT13 0QN
Nearest station: Weybridge

Wander through Abbotsbury Swannery

The only place in the world where it is possible to walk through a colony of nesting mute swans is Abbotsbury Swannery. It was established around the westerly end of the Fleet Lagoon by the monks of nearby Abbotsbury Abbey at least as early as the fourteenth century, in order to harvest swan meat for their lavish Dorset banquets.

While the monks were forced out with the dissolution of the monasteries in the sixteenth century, the swans still return, and between the end of May and the end of June, up to 1,000 swans nest and hatch their chicks. It is a spectacular sight, and the paths that meander through the Swannery allow visitors to get close to the nesting birds and their young cygnets.

Website: www.abbotsbury-tourism.co.uk/swannery.htm
Address: New Barn Road, Abbotsbury, Dorset DT3 4JG
Nearest station: Weymouth

See the Sunrise at Avebury

While crowds gather to mark Midsummer at nearby Stonehenge, the summer solstice at Avebury is a much more civilised affair. The village sits at the heart of Avebury's Neolithic stone circle, and the area is owned and managed by the National Trust.

Along with Stonehenge, the standing stones at Avebury, which are thought to be over 4,000 years old, are designated as a UNESCO World Heritage Site. At Midsummer, druids, hippies and locals gather for a joyous celebration of the season.

Website: www.nationaltrust.org.uk/avebury/
Address: Avebury, Nr Marlborough, Wiltshire
Nearest station: Pewsey; Swindon

Attend the Appleby Horse Fair

Taking place every June in the Cumbrian town of Appleby-in-Westmorland, the Appleby Horse Fair is led by gypsy and traveller communities, who come to the town for an annual celebration based on a horse-trading fair. The 10,000 or so traditional attendees are joined by around 30,000 visitors descending on a town of just 2,500 people.

The fair has taken place since at least 1685, when the town was granted a charter to host it by James II, and continues to be hugely popular. An iconic sight of the fair each year is the bathing of horses in the River Eden, which runs through the town, as owners get ready to show and sell them.

Website: www.applebyfair.org/
Address: Various locations in Appleby
Nearest station: Appleby

Await King Arthur at Cadbury Castle

Each year, on Midsummer Night, Arthur and the Knights of the Round Table are said to ride over the hilltop at Cadbury Castle in Somerset, passing through the castle's gateway to allow their horses to drink at a spring beside Sutton Montis church. Visitors have reported hearing ghostly hoof beats.

An Iron Age hill fort, thought to be around 3,000 years old, the castle has been cited as a possible location of King Arthur's mysterious Camelot, and the first written record of this legend dates from the sixteenth century.

Website: www.visitsomerset.co.uk
Address: South Cadbury, Somerset
Nearest station: Castle Cary; Templecombe

Learn to Surf at Saltburn

Although surfing is more usually associated with the beaches of Cornwall – or California – surfers have been riding the waves at Saltburn-by-the-Sea, on the North Sea coast near Middlesbrough, for more than forty years.

By 1983 the surfing scene had grown to such a degree that Saltburn Surf was able to set up in the town, and today the only East Coast surf school approved by Surfing Great Britain offers lessons on the beach, as well as the hire of boards and near-mandatory wetsuits to help surfers combat the icy waters.

Website: www.saltburnsurf.co.uk/
Address: Lower Promenade, Saltburn-by-the-Sea, Cleveland TS12 1HQ
Nearest station: Saltburn

Take a Boat from Windermere's Bowness Pier

Hiring a boat on Lake Windermere – England's largest lake – is one of the Lake District's simplest pleasures, with rowing boats and motor launches available for hire by the hour, and larger boats offering cruises further afield.

The smaller boats allow visitors to explore at their own pace, and offer the opportunity to recreate the adventures of the heroes of Arthur Ransome's *Swallows and Amazons*, which helped to bring boating in the Lake District to the popular consciousness.

Website: www.visitcumbria.com/amb/bowness-on-windermere
Address: Bowness-on-Windermere, Cumbria, LA23 3HQ
Nearest station: Windermere

See the Derbyshire Well Dressings

The ancient art of well dressing is alive and well in the Peak District, and each summer from May to September, the wells of towns and villages around the region are dressed with flowers in a ritual of uncertain origin – possibly a pagan tradition, or even a reaction to the impurities of the Black Death.

In June, many wells across the county are dressed, with colourful wooden frames erected and decorated with materials such as flower petals, berries and moss. Meanwhile, in towns and villages such as Wirksworth, Whaley, Hope and Bakewell, carnivals are organised to coincide with the well dressings, adding to the festivities of the season.

Website: http://welldressing.com/
Address: Various locations across Derbyshire
Nearest station: Chesterfield; Frome; Haslemere; Hope and more

Attend the Glastonbury Festival

In 1970, young farmer Michael Eavis was so inspired by his experience crawling through a hedge to see Led Zeppelin at the Bath Blues Festival that he decided to stage something similar at his own farm to try to pay off his mortgage. Despite the financial failure of the first festival, it seized the imagination of a group of hippies led by Andrew Kerr and Arabella Churchill, Winston Churchill's granddaughter, who returned the following year to ensure the festival took place.

More than forty years later, the Glastonbury Festival has become an institution, with more than 150,000 attendees annually, and a reputation for artistic, musical and environmental innovation that makes it a driving force in national culture, despite occasional muddy interludes.

Website: www.glastonburyfestivals.co.uk
Address: Glastonbury, Somerset
Nearest station: Castle Cary

WATCH THE DURHAM MINERS' GALA PARADE

A tradition dating back to 1871, when the Durham Miners' Association organised the first event, the Durham Miners' Gala once attracted up to 300,000 people for a day of banner parades, brass bands and speeches, and still brings around 50,000 visitors to the town, making it one of Britain's largest political gatherings.

Despite the decline of mining in the Durham coalfields, the gala continues to be important to unionists and local residents, with many travelling to the town to see the bright banners of lodges of the National Union of Mineworkers and others, and to enjoy the music of up to fifty brass bands parading through the streets.

Website: http://durhamminers.org/
Address: Durham City Market Place
Nearest station: Durham

Watch the Cornish Midsummer Bonfires

An ancient Cornish tradition is observed each year on 23 June, with bonfires lit across the county to mark St John's Day and the coming of midsummer.

The Old Cornwall Societies of St Just in Penwith, Redruth, Madron, St Columb Major and St Ives are at the forefront of this enduring tradition, with the first fire often lit at Chapel Carn Brea near Land's End, England's most westerly hill.

Website: www.oldcornwall.org/midsummer_bonfire.htm
Address: Various locations across Cornwall
Nearest station: Redruth

Search for Robin Hood in Sherwood Forest

Today, Sherwood Forest covers a fraction of the area it would have done when the legend of Robin Hood emerged in popular folklore, but it is still possible to find a quiet part of the 450-acre country park to imagine his band of merry men planning their raids.

The most famous spot associated with Robin Hood is the Major Oak, a huge oak tree believed to be around 800 years old. It is said the hollow trunk was used by Hood and his men as a hideout, and while there is no proof for this story, the tree is recognised for its part in English culture.

Website: www.sherwoodforest.org.uk
Address: Sherwood Forest Visitor Centre, Swinecote Road, Edwinstowe, Nottinghamshire, NG21 9HN
Nearest station: Newark Northgate; Nottingham

Stay at Greg's Hut

Found in the shadow of Cross Fell – the highest mountain in England outside the Lake District – Greg's Hut is a basic stone shelter that has been providing a stop for the walkers of the North Pennines for decades, with a free stretch of bare floor for anyone who arrives by foot, which they mostly do along the Pennine Way.

One of only a handful of bothies in Northern England, the hut is maintained by the volunteers of the Mountain Bothy Association, a charity established in 1965 and which now maintains more than 100 such shelters, most of them in the wilds of Scotland.

Website: http://www.culgaith.org.uk/Ghut.html
Address: Greg's Hut, Cross Fell, the Pennine Way
Nearest station: Langwathby

Go on Safari at Longleat

Opened in 1966 on the Marquess of Bath's 900-acre Longleat Estate, Longleat Safari Park was the first such landscape outside Africa, offering visitors the chance to drive through animal enclosures in a simulation of the African savannah.

Famed for its lion park – which caused outrage when it was opened, with locals fearful of lions running wild in the Wiltshire countryside – the park is home to a wide range of animals, including giraffes, zebras, rhinos and tigers.

Website: www.longleat.co.uk
Address: Longleat, Warminster, Wiltshire, BA12 7NW
Nearest station: Warminster

Visit William Morris's Summer Home

In the summer of 1871, Arts and Crafts movement leader William Morris and Pre-Raphaelite painter Dante Gabriel Rossetti signed a joint lease to rent Kelmscott Manor, a sixteenth-century Cotswold stone house close to the Thames in Oxfordshire, which Morris described as 'a heaven on earth', and which remained his summer home until the end of his life in 1896.

In June, it is not difficult to see why Morris was so inspired by Kelmscott, close to nature with its beautiful gardens in bloom, and the rustic charm of the village and meadows beyond. As a tribute to Morris, the manor is now maintained by the Society of Antiquaries of London, and open to the public on Wednesdays and Sundays in summer.

Website: www.kelmscottmanor.co.uk
Address: Kelmscott Manor, Kelmscott, Lechlade, Glos., GL7 3HJ
Nearest station: Swindon; Oxford

See the Place where Magna Carta was Signed

Following lengthy negotiations with the nobles, King John finally came to Runnymede in June 1215 to put his seal on the Magna Carta. The document – which marked the first time a king had signed up to follow the laws of the land and recognise the rights of free individuals – was a significant step for liberty in England, and is still regarded as an important part of the country's unwritten constitution.

In recognition of its important role in English history, Runnymede is maintained by the National Trust, to which it was donated in 1929, and various memorials are dotted across its hundreds of acres of water meadows and woodland, including the Magna Carta Memorial, a domed classical temple containing a pillar of English granite.

Website: www.nationaltrust.org.uk/runnymede
Address: Lower slopes of Cooper's Hill, Runnymede
Nearest station: Egham

July

At its best a month of long, sunny, hazy days, July sees fields slowly turn golden brown and holidays begin. The arrival of the full Hay Moon is the traditional time for haymaking, and the month was referred to by the Anglo-Saxons as Heymonath or Hay-month.

However, July can occasionally be the wettest month of the season, so nothing is certain; by the middle of the month, St Swithin's Day is make-or-break for the rest of the summer, with folklore dictating the weather on the 15th will continue for the next forty days. Whatever the weather, the English persevere in July, with cricket matches, picnics, days at the beach and the gathering of summer fruits.

WATCH THE CRICKET AT BROAD-HALFPENNY DOWN

The world's first cricket club was formed in Hambledon in Hampshire in the mid-eighteenth century, playing at Broadhalfpenny Down, where team member Richard Nyren was landlord of the Bat & Ball, and the club established its headquarters.

Though the original Hambledon Club moved its matches to nearby Windmill Down in 1781, play was resumed at Broadhalfpenny Down in 1908, when a Hambledon vs England XI match featured legendary cricketer C B Fry and was watched by W G Grace. Today, the place known as the 'cradle of cricket' is home to the Broadhalfpenny Brigands Cricket Club, whose matches can still be watched from the beer garden at the Bat & Ball.

Website: www.broadhalfpennydown.com
Address: Hambledon, Hampshire
Nearest station: Portchester; Cosham; Rowlands Castle

Attend the Goodwood Festival of Speed

An annual celebration of the history of motorcars, the Goodwood Festival of Speed is held in early July, or occasionally in late June, and attracts over 100,000 people to the grounds of Goodwood House in Sussex.

The event is known for its garden-party atmosphere, and offers a chance to see famous faces from the past and present of motor racing, and to watch races between vintage cars.

Website: www.goodwood.co.uk/festival-of-speed
Address: Goodwood, West Sussex
Nearest station: Chichester

See Durdle Door

One of Dorset's most recognisable features, situated a short distance from beautiful Lulworth Cove in Dorset, is Durdle Door, a natural limestone arch carved out over 140 million years by the lashing of countless waves.

The Door sits on a stretch of coastline that, from the sea at least, seems largely unspoilt, and maintains its natural beauty. This is just a very pleasant illusion, however, as behind the cliffs sits a holiday park – thankfully not visible from the beautiful beaches.

Website: www.durdledoor.org.uk
Address: West Lulworth, Wareham, Dorset
Nearest station: Weymouth

See an Exhibition at the Baltic

On Saturday, 13 July 2002, the Baltic Centre for Contemporary Art opened its doors at the Baltic Flour Mill, a huge industrial space built in 1950 by Rank Hovis on the south bank of the River Tyne.

With no permanent collection, the Baltic now hosts a changing programme of artistic exhibitions and events across four gallery spaces, and is recognised as a major international centre for contemporary art.

Website: www.balticmill.com
Address: Gateshead Quays, South Shore Road, Gateshead NE8 3BA
Nearest station: Newcastle Central

Watch the Polo at Cowdray Park

The polo season lasts from May to September. By July, it is in full swing at Cowdray Park Polo Club, near Midhurst in Sussex, one of England's leading polo clubs, where spectator tickets can be bought at the gate for a small charge.

Polo has been played at Cowdray Park, the 16,500-acre country estate of Viscount Cowdray, for more than a century. The highlight of the season is the annual Gold Cup, which lasts until mid-July.

Website: www.cowdraypolo.co.uk
Address: Easebourne, Midhurst GU29 0AJ
Nearest station: Haslemere; Pulborough

Relive the Telling of Alice's Adventures

In early July 1862, Charles Lutwidge Dodgson set off on a summer outing in a hired rowing boat from Folly Bridge in Oxford along the Isis towards Godstow. Among those in his party were the three young daughters of the Dean of Christ Church College, Alice, Lorina and Edith Liddell, and Dodgson entertained them with a story he created on the spur of the moment for ten-year-old Alice.

The story was such a success that Dodgson later committed it to paper, publishing *Alice's Adventures in Wonderland* under the pseudonym Lewis Carroll three years later. Boats are still available to hire at Folly Bridge, offering a chance to recreate the voyage, and copies of the novel are available from the original Blackwell's bookshop in Broad Street.

Website: www.salterssteamers.co.uk
Address: Folly Bridge, Oxford
Nearest station: Oxford

Explore Dover's Secret Tunnels

Deep beneath Dover Castle, burrowed through the famous White Cliffs themselves, a network of secret tunnels became England's front line after Second World War troops returned from Dunkirk in 1940, and it was from here that Admiral Ramsay coordinated the mass evacuation of Dunkirk.

During the War, the tunnels contained an operations room, a telephone exchange, a barracks for the Women's Auxiliary Air Force and even an underground hospital. During the Cold War, they were put to use again, and even expanded to provide a regional base for the government in the event of a nuclear attack.

Website: www.english-heritage.org.uk/daysout/properties/
dover-castle
Address: Castle Hill Road, Dover, Kent CT16 1HU
Nearest station: Dover

REMEMBER THE TOLPUDDLE MARTYRS

The Dorset village of Tolpuddle is synonymous with the struggle of the Tolpuddle Martyrs, a group of farm workers who, living on meagre wages during the nineteenth century, formed the Friendly Society of Agricultural Labourers to protest against the lowering of pay. It resulted in their arrest for swearing an illegal oath and their transportation to Australia.

The Martyrs eventually had their sentence remitted after huge public support for their cause, with a demonstration marching through London and 800,000 people signing a petition to Parliament. An annual festival is now held in Tolpuddle each July to remember the struggle, and to allow activists to engage in political discussion, hear speeches, and listen to music and engage in other activities, culminating in a procession through the village.

Website: www.tolpuddlemartyrs.org.uk
Address: Tolpuddle Martyrs Museum, Tolpuddle DT2 7EH
Nearest station: Moreton

Wild Camp on Dartmoor

One of a very few spots in England where free camping is permitted, Dartmoor is a rare example of the remaining truly wild landscape.

Camping among the rolling moorland, and awakening to vast skies, is a great way to feel in touch with nature, and as long as you pitch your tent discreetly, at least 100 metres from the road, and away from people's homes and restricted areas, it is completely legal and free.

Website: www.dartmoor-npa.gov.uk
Address: Parke, Bovey Tracey, Newton Abbot, Devon TQ13 9JQ
Nearest station: Dartmoor

Stay in Alde Garden

A campsite with a difference, Alde Garden in Sweffling, Suffolk, is set in a peaceful one-acre wildlife garden, with facilities ranging from traditional bring-your-own camping to a yurt, tipi, gypsy caravan and small cottage.

The environmentally friendly site is in the grounds of the Sweffling White Horse Inn, which provides food and drink for those seeking an evening indoors, or a communal campfire for those wanting to spend the night under the stars. The site also offers a kitchen, an outdoor pizza oven, a herb garden and free bike hire.

Website: www.aldegarden.co.uk
Address: The White Horse Inn, Low Road, Sweffling, Suffolk IP17 2BB
Nearest station: Saxmundham

Attend the Beggars Fair

An annual free festival of music and dance in Romsey, Hampshire, with a particular focus on local musicians, the Beggars Fair has been a summer fixture for over twenty years.

As well as jazz, folk, blues and world music, and dance on stages at the Cornmarket and in the Memorial Park, the festival sees acoustic music in pubs, churches and other venues.

Website: www.beggars-fair.org.uk
Address: Romsey, Hampshire
Nearest station: Romsey

Go Swimming in Pells Pool

First built in 1860, Pells Pool in Lewes, Sussex, is the oldest freshwater swimming pool in England. It was built for the use of all local swimmers on land originally donated to the townspeople in 1603.

The open-air lido is now a Grade II-listed structure, and was saved from closure during the late 1990s following a number of plans to shut it down. The pool is now run by volunteers in the form of the Pells Pool Community Association.

Website: www.pellspool.org.uk
Address: The Pells Pool, Brook Street, Lewes, East Sussex BN7 2BA
Nearest station: Lewes

Drink Cornish Tea

The private estate of Tregothnan, near Truro in Cornwall, is the home of England's only tea plantation, thanks to a climate similar to that of the high foothills of the Himalayas. Owned by the Boscawen family since 1335, the estate first grew ornamental Camellia – from the same family as the tea plant – around 200 years ago, and since 2000 has been the home of English tea.

Though the tea plantations are not open to the public, they can occasionally be visited on private garden visits, which can be booked directly. The estate also runs lectures and tutored tea tastings, as well as serving tea at the on-site Smugglers Restaurant and Tea Bar.

Website: tregothnan.co.uk/smugglers
Address: The Woodyard, Tresillian, Truro, Cornwall TR2 4AJ
Nearest station: Truro

Watch for Ships from Plymouth Hoe

A distinctive ridge with sweeping views across the important natural harbour of Plymouth, the Hoe has been vital to English naval strategy since well before – as legend has it – Sir Francis Drake played bowls here while waiting for the tide to change in July 1588 so that he could set off to battle the Spanish Armada.

Down on the dockside, the Mayflower Steps mark the point from which the Pilgrim Fathers are believed to have boarded the *Mayflower* to begin their journey to the New World. The surrounding Barbican area – one of the few parts of Plymouth to escape destruction during the Second World War – offers a glimpse of what the city would have been like in an earlier age.

Website: www.visitplymouth.co.uk
Address: The Hoe, Plymouth
Nearest station: Plymouth

Watch the Butterflies on Fontwell and Melbury Downs

The chalk downland around Melbury Abbas in Dorset is one of England's richest areas for butterflies, whose season is in full swing in July. Compton Down and Melbury Hill also provide a good habitat for glow-worms, which sometimes provide a unique nighttime display at this time of year.

The hills are home to some thirty-five species of butterfly, including marsh fritillary, chalkhill and Adonis blues, and are protected by the National Trust for their natural importance. They were purchased in memory of the writer Thomas Hardy, who took inspiration from the area.

Website: www.nationaltrust.org.uk/fontmell-and-melbury-downs
Address: Melbury Abbas, Dorset
Nearest station: Gillingham

ATTEND AN EXHIBITION AT THE DE LA WARR PAVILION

The De La Warr Pavilion, standing on the seafront in the Sussex town of Bexhill-on-Sea, is an icon of the Modernist age, and is Grade I-listed by English Heritage. Commissioned by the ninth Earl De La Warr in 1935, the Pavilion was designed by Erich Mendelsohn and Serge Chermayeff, and was the first Modernist public building in England.

Reopened in 2005 following extensive refurbishment, the Pavilion today has two contemporary galleries, which host a range of thought-provoking exhibitions, and a huge auditorium, which is a venue for live shows.

Website: www.dlwp.com
Address: Marina, Bexhill on Sea, East Sussex TN40 1DP
Nearest station: Bexhill

Descend into the Hellfire Caves

The venue for the aristocrat Francis Dashwood's notorious drinking society, the Hellfire Caves are a quarter-mile network of caves dug into the hillside above West Wycombe in Buckinghamshire.

The caves extend through a number of chambers to the Inner Temple, where meetings of the Hellfire Club were held, passing a banqueting hall, the River Styx and a chamber named after Benjamin Franklin, who once visited. At their furthest point, the caves are some 300 metres below St Lawrence's Church on the hillside above.

Website: www.hellfirecaves.co.uk
Address: Church Lane, W. Wycombe, High Wycombe, Bucks. HP14 3AH
Nearest station: High Wycombe

Canoe the River Wye

There are a number of stretches of the River Wye that are possible to canoe in a day, and one of the most popular is the area around Symonds Yat, where a limestone outcrop rises around 500 feet from the riverbank, offering spectacular scenery.

For those looking for a more sedate spot, Hereford Canoe Hire operates along one of the most picturesque parts of the river between Hereford and Ross-on-Wye, where novices and families can enjoy a day afloat, going with the flow as green fields and wooded hills roll by.

Website: www.herefordcanoehire.com
Address: Lucksall Park, Mordiford, Hereford, Herefordshire HR1 4LP
Nearest station: Hereford

Listen for Trewella's Song at Pendour Cove

A local legend in the village of Zennor on the North Cornwall coast tells of a beautiful woman who made irregular visits to the village church and so impressed Mathey Trewella, the best singer in the congregation, that he fell in love with her, followed her out to sea and never returned.

The legend of Trewella is kept alive in the village in the form of a carved oak pew (*above*) in the beautiful church of Saint Senara, and it is said that, when sitting above Pendour Cove at sunset on a fine summer's evening, one can still occasionally hear Trewella's beautiful singing drifting across the waves.

Website: www.achurchnearyou.com/zennor-st-senara
Address: Saint Senara's Church, Zennor, St Ives, Cornwall TR26 3BY
Nearest station: St Ives

Take a Boat on the Norfolk Broads

The Norfolk Broads, the result of hundreds of years of peat extraction begun by the Romans and continued as Norfolk grew richer during the Middle Ages, are arguably the best place in England to hire a boat. The Broads boast 125 miles of navigable waterways, connecting picturesque villages and friendly local inns with market towns and the sea beyond.

The area has been popular for boating since 1878, when local man John Loynes started hiring boats to friends. Loynes's boatyard at Wroxham – one of the oldest on the Broads – is still operating today, allowing visitors access to an area rich in wildlife and natural beauty.

Website: www.norfolkbroadsdirect.co.uk/about-your-holiday-cruiser
Address: The Bridge, Norwich Road, Wroxham, Norfolk NR12 8RX
Nearest station: Wroxham

Eat Oysters at Whitstable

Oysters were first exported from the North Kent coast to Rome in around AD 80, and the area around Whitstable has been known for its oysters ever since. By the Norman period – when Whitstable was already well established as a fishing port – oyster fishermen and dredgers held annual ceremonies of thanksgiving for their survival and harvest.

The town still gives thanks for its catch with an annual Oyster Festival, a 1980s revival that embraces the history and heritage of earlier celebrations, as the people of the town gather to celebrate a mollusc that has given wealth to Whitstable for nearly 2,000 years.

Website: www.whitstableoysterfestival.co.uk
Address: Whistable, Kent
Nearest station: Whistable

Stay in a Beach Hut
on Mudeford Spit

A spit of sand at the entrance to Christchurch Harbour in Dorset, Mudeford Spit is home to a tightly packed community of more than 300 beach huts, which offer visitors an overnight escape from the rigours of modern living.

The huts are accessed by ferry from central Christchurch, and from March to November provide temporary homes for those looking for a holiday with a difference: facing right onto the beach but staying in a small hut with access only to communal toilets and showers, and no hot water.

Website: www.mudeford-beach-huts.co.uk
Address: The Spit, Mudeford, Christchurch, Dorset BH23 3ND
Nearest station: Hengistbury Head

EXPLORE BARBARA HEPWORTH'S HOME

Though the great twentieth-century sculptor Barbara Hepworth was born in Wakefield in Yorkshire and spent time in Hampstead in London, and Italy, she eventually settled in St Ives in Cornwall with her husband, Ben Nicholson, in 1939. Here, in 1949, Hepworth acquired a traditional stone building called Trewyn Studios, where she worked until she was killed in a fire in the building in 1975.

The building that had become Hepworth's home, was opened to the public – according to her wishes – in 1976, and remains open all year round, allowing visitors the opportunity to see the place where Hepworth lived and worked. Take time to explore the beautiful garden she created with her friend, the South African-born composer, Priaulx Rainier, who helped plant it with exotic plants.

Website: www.tate.org.uk/visit/tate-st-ives/barbara-hepworth-museum
Address: Barnoon Hill, St Ives, Cornwall TR26 1AD
Nearest station: St Ives

Drink a 'Pint' of Clarion Tea

Founded in 1912 for the use of members of the Independent Labour Party, the Clarion House is located on a quiet lane in a hidden valley in the shadow of Lancashire's Pendle Hill, and is still offering tea, cake and left-wing politics to walkers and cyclists over a century later.

Open every Sunday, the Clarion House was once one of several such buildings, designed to give workers from nearby industrial towns the chance to escape from their smoky environs and to spend a day in the countryside, a philosophy it retains to this day.

Website: www.clarionhouse.org.uk
Address: Clarion House, Jinney Lane, Newchurch-in-Pendle BB12 9LL
Nearest station: Brierfield and Nelson

Attend the Cambridge Folk Festival

Each July, the Cambridge Folk Festival brings the great and the good of the world of folk music to Cambridge for a music festival in the park at Cherry Hinton Hall, on the outskirts of the city.

The festival has been running since the 1960s, and, as well as traditional folk acts, attracts musicians from other genres to perform in an event renowned for its relaxed atmosphere.

Website: www.cambridgefolkfestival.co.uk
Address: Cherry Hinton Hall, Cherry Hinton Road, Cambridge CB1 8DW
Nearest station: Cambridge

Explore Beer Quarry Caves

First exploited by the Romans, and still being quarried in 1900, the Quarry Caves at Beer in Devon have provided stone for Windsor Castle and Westminster Abbey, and extend for miles beneath the limestone hillside.

The stone was prized by stonemasons, as it was malleable when first quarried and only hardened when exposed to fresh air, which made it easy to carve. The location was particularly prized as the caves are close to the sea, where the stone could be loaded onto ships for transport.

Website: www.beerquarrycaves.co.uk
Address: Quarry Lane, Beer, Devon EX12 3AT
Nearest station: Seaton

Play Croquet at the Bishop's Palace

The Bishop's Palace at Wells in Somerset has been home to the Bishops of Bath and Wells for 800 years. Within its fourteen acres lies St Andrew's Well, after which the city is named.

In addition to being an important visitor attraction, and providing a home for the Bishop, the palace is home to the Palace Croquet Club, which runs regular beginners' sessions on the immaculate croquet lawn.

Website: www.bishopspalacewells.co.uk
Address: The Bishops Palace, Wells, Somerset, BA5 2PD
Nearest station: Castle Cary

Visit Jane Austen's House

In July 1809, following an unhappy few years at Bath, marked by the death of her father, Jane Austen returned with her mother and sisters to Hampshire, to live in a cottage (*below*) in the village of Chawton, on an estate recently inherited by her brother, Edward.

Austen was to spend most of the final eight years of her life at Chawton and it was here that her literary career finally started to make headway, as she wrote *Emma*, *Mansfield Park* and *Persuasion* and revisited *Sense and Sensibility*, *Pride and Prejudice* and *Northanger Abbey*. The cottage is now a museum to Jane Austen's work, and contains items relating to Austen's life, such as her tiny writing desk and the tea-and-coffee cupboard to which she held the key.

Website: www.jane-austens-house-museum.org.uk
Address: Chawton, Alton, Hampshire GU34 1SD
Nearest station: Alton

See Durham by Rowing Boat

Browns Rowing Boats provide a relaxing way to see Durham; available to hire by the hour from the riverside close to Elvet Bridge in the city centre.

From here, boaters can head upstream to the Bandstand and Durham Cow – a statue that references the Dun Cow, which guided the monks of Lindisfarne to the spot where they founded the city in AD 995 – or float downstream and admire the views of the castle and cathedral.

Website: www.princebishoprc.co.uk/rowingboats
Address: Boat Ho, Elvet Bridge, Durham DH1 3AF
Nearest station: Durham

Cross the Causeway to St Michael's Mount

The striking tidal island that dominates Mount's Bay in Cornwall is steeped in timeless mystery. Mythologised as the home of the giant Cormoran, it is said to be named after Archangel Michael who appeared to fishermen here in AD 495.

By the time of the Norman Conquest, an abbey had stood on the site for hundreds of years. In the eleventh century, it was granted to the Benedictine monks of Mont St Michel, a twin island in Brittany. The island has been in the hands of the St Aubyn family since the seventeenth century.

Website: www.stmichaelsmount.co.uk
Address: St Michael's Mount, Marazion, Cornwall, TR17 0HS
Nearest station: Penzance

GO ON A PILGRIMAGE
TO ST PETER'S CHAPEL

The Chapel of St Peter-on-the-Wall, near Bradwell-on-Sea in Essex, was established on the site of a Roman fort in AD 654, by St Cedd, a monk who arrived from Lindisfarne at the request of King Sigbert of the East Saxons. Though Cedd's original chapel is thought to have been made from wood, he soon constructed a stone one on the same site using Roman bricks from the nearby fort of Othona.

The current church is thought to date from around AD 660, and still makes use of the original Roman bricks. Today, the chapel is a popular place of pilgrimage for Christians and others, and as well as being the subject of an annual pilgrimage in July, it stands at the end of the St Peter's Way, a forty-five-mile walk through Essex from Chipping Ongar.

Website: www.bradwellchapel.org
Address: The Rectory, East End Road, Bradwell-on-Sea, Essex CM0 7PX
Nearest station: Southminster

August

August is a holiday month, with schools empty and workplaces quieter as workers head to beaches and hills with their families for a well-earned rest. Towns and villages around the coast and countryside fill with new faces; warm seas make way for swimming and surfing, while sails appear on the horizon.

The first day of the month is Lammastide, traditionally marking the start of harvest with the cutting of the first corn and the gathering of the new crop, and with the arrival of the Corn Moon the days are already getting shorter, especially in the far North. However, a rich crop of apples and hedges filled with blackberries help stave off the change, and good weather usually continues.

WALK IN FIELDS OF NORFOLK LAVENDER

Founded in 1932, Norfolk Lavender is one of the country's biggest lavender farms. It covers around 100 acres of fields, which bloom from the middle of June until the end of August, offering a beautiful display of colour in the North Norfolk countryside.

The farm, found in the coastal village of Heacham, is also home to a lavender-oil distillery (which has been producing lavender oil since the 1930s) and the National Collection of Lavenders, a collection of over 100 varieties of lavender, which it runs in association with Plant Heritage.

Website: www.norfolk-lavender.co.uk
Address: Caley Mill, Lynn Rd, King's Lynn, Norfolk PE31 7JE
Nearest station: Heacham

Visit Scolt Head, England's Desert Island

A tranquil island of white sands and quiet beaches on the North Norfolk coast, Scolt Head Island is sometimes known as England's only desert island, thanks in large part to its main northerly beach, which is backed by a ridge of sand dunes.

Elsewhere, the island is known for its saltmarshes, which are some of the finest in the country, as well as the best documented in the world.

Website: www.naturalengland.org
Address: Scolt Head Island NNR, Norfolk
Nearest station: Sheringham

Watch the Yachts of Cowes Week

Britain's longest-running regatta has been held at Cowes, on the Isle of Wight, since 1826, and today attracts up to 1,000 boats and around 100,000 spectators.

As well as scores of yacht races, the event sees a range of entertainment on dry land, with food, drink, music and fireworks, and a festive atmosphere in the town, culminating in the annual fireworks display, which has been taking place for more than 150 years.

Website: www.cowes.co.uk
Address: Cowes, Isle of Wight
Nearest station: Southhampton

Ride the Anderton Boat Lift

Known locally as the 'Cathedral of Canals', the Anderton Boat Lift in Anderton, near Northwich in Cheshire, was built in 1875 to lift boats fifty feet between the River Weaver and the Trent and Mersey Canal.

The only such lift in England, the Anderton runs regular boat trips in August, and also has a visitors' centre explaining its fascinating history.

Website: www.andertonboatlift.co.uk
Address: Lift Lane, Anderton, Northwich, Cheshire CW9 6FW
Nearest station: Northwich

Follow the Queen's Guide to the Sands

An official guide has been leading walkers across the sands of Morecambe Bay, between Arnside and Grange-over-Sands, since long before the current railway bridge was built, using local knowledge to cross the potentially dangerous and ever-changing tidal estuary for centuries.

A Queen's Guide to the Sands is still appointed by the Duchy of Lancaster, and leads guided walks of around eight miles between May and September each year.

Website: www.arnside-online.co.uk
Address: Arnside Promenade, Cumbria
Nearest station: Arnside

Spend the Night at Black Sail Hostel

A favourite with Lakeland walkers for more than seventy-five years, the tiny Black Sail Hut sits miles from any road in the wild valley of Ennerdale, in the shadow of the peaks of Great Gable, Kirk Fell, Pillar and Haystacks, and accessible over high mountain passes.

Once a shepherds' bothy and now operated by the Youth Hostel Association, Black Sail offers just sixteen bunks and outdoor toilets. It offers the experience of being in a real mountain hut, with the communal lounge a place to reflect on the day's walking, and to dry off on days when the weather does not meet expectations, as well as an unrivalled view of the stars away from civilisation on a clear night.

Website: www.yha.org.uk/hostel/black-sail
Address: Black Sail Hut, Ennerdale, Cleator, Cumbria CA23 3AY
Nearest station: Dalegarth

Go Messing About in Boats

The sleepy stretch of the River Thames between Henley and Windsor was the inspiration for Kenneth Grahame's *Wind in the Willows*, and the setting for Ratty's assertion that, 'There is NOTHING, absolute nothing, half so much worth doing as simply messing about in boats.' It also featured in Jerome K Jerome's river-borne classic *Three Men in a Boat*.

Boats are available to hire on summer's days from Higginson Park in Marlow or Hobbs of Henley, allowing even the most ordinary inhabitant of the Wild Wood the chance to get afloat for an hour or so, and to enjoy some of the most beautiful stretches of the Thames.

Website: www.hobbs-of-henley.com
Address: Station Road, Henley-on-Thames, Oxfordshire RG9 1AZ
Nearest station: Henley

EXPLORE THE BIRTHPLACE OF THE SCOUTS

At the beginning of August 1907, Robert Baden-Powell brought together the first Scout camp on Brownsea Island in Poole Harbour, as a test of the ideas he had put forward in his book *Scouting for Boys*. Today, the island is in the care of the National Trust, and is open to the public via Brownsea Island Ferries, which have been transporting visitors across the bay for more than 100 years.

Brownsea is a peaceful place, a world away from the hustle and bustle of the mainland, and, as home to the Baden-Powell Outdoor Centre, still maintains a strong association with the Scouting movement. It is also notable as a nature reserve and, along with the Isle of Wight, is one of the few places in Southern England where red squirrels can still be found in the wild.

Website: www.nationaltrust.org.uk/brownsea-island
Address: Poole Harbour, Poole, BH13 7EE
Nearest station: Poole

Visit Helston Folk Museum

A fine museum in the Cornish market town of Helston, the Helston Folk Museum is surprisingly large. Containing collections reflecting many aspects of life in a town with a small population but a proud heritage, it certainly puts many London museums to shame.

The rather ramshackle collection tells the story of the little Cornish town through artefacts such as a huge cider press, the paperwork and photographs of the town's first motorcar, and various items of folk and smuggling history on the Cornish coast.

Website: www.museumsincornwall.org.uk
Address: Market Place, Helston, Cornwall TR13 8TH
Nearest station: Redruth

Attend the Notting Hill Carnival

One of the world's largest street parties, the Notting Hill Carnival in West London sees people from all over London and the country – led by the West Indian community – take to the streets in a celebration to end the summer.

Held on the August Bank Holiday each year since 1966, it is the largest carnival in Europe and the second largest in the world, with twenty miles of parades, forty static sound systems, 40,000 volunteers and up to a million carnival revellers.

Website: www.thenottinghillcarnival.com
Address: Notting Hill, London
Nearest underground station: Notting Hill; Queensway; Bayswater

Watch Lakeland Sports in Grasmere

For more than 160 years, the village of Grasmere in the Lake District has been hosting an annual Lakeland Sports show, demonstrating the arts of fell running, hound trailing, Cumberland wrestling and other local pastimes.

The event still takes place each August in the show field in Grasmere, combining traditional sports with bird-of-prey displays, sheepdog trials, marching bands, a tug-of-war, and local food and drink, including local speciality Grasmere Gingerbread.

Website: www.grasmeresports.com
Address: The Showfield, Stock Lane Grasmere, Cumbria LA22 9SL
Nearest station: Grasmere

Drink at the Berney Arms

A sleepy place on the banks of the River Yare, popular with boaters and walkers, the Berney Arms is a pub in a hamlet of the same name. The pub is accessible by boat, a three-and-a-half-mile walk from Halvergate, or by rare train to the hamlet's own Berney Arms Station, which is a request stop on the Norwich–Great Yarmouth line.

Nearby, the Berney Arms Mill and Windpump, the tallest windmill in Norfolk, stands peacefully. Now in the care of English Heritage, it can be visited on pre-booked tours. Together with the RSPB reserve of Berney Marshes, the area offers a pleasant place to while away half a day or so.

Website: http://www.berneyarms.co.uk
Address: Berney Arms, Great Yarmouth, Norfolk NR30 1SB
Nearest station: Berney Arms

Explore the Yorkshire Sculpture Park

England's first permanent sculpture park – Yorkshire Sculpture Park – was opened to the public in 1977. Occupying 500 acres of rolling parkland around Bretton Hall in West Yorkshire, the park is at its best on summer afternoons, offering a vast art gallery in a grand setting.

Pieces by local sculptors Henry Moore, Barbara Hepworth and others attract over 300,000 visitors annually, with the sense of space and fresh air making for an invigorating experience. There are also exhibitions in indoor spaces such as the Bothy Gallery, the Underground Gallery and the Longside Gallery, offering a haven in the event of inclement weather.

Website: www.ysp.co.uk
Address: West Bretton, Wakefield, West Yorkshire WF4 4LG
Nearest station: Wakefield Westgate

Find Betjeman's Final Resting Place

During childhood visits the late poet Sir John Betjeman fell in love with the chapel of St Enodoc (*above*), a building tracing its history back to the twelfth century. Standing among sand dunes on the north coast of Cornwall, and overlooking Daymer Bay and the Doom Bar, the chapel was once buried in sand dunes and accessible only for annual services via a hole in the roof.

When the sands eventually receded, new life was breathed into St Enodoc's, and the chapel was renovated in 1864. This is the way Betjeman came to know and love it, first as a child, and later when he immortalised it in his poem about the village of Trebetherick. Upon his death, Betjeman chose to be laid to rest in the graveyard, where his grave can still be found.

Website: www.stendellion.org.uk/st_enodoc
Address: Trebetherick, St Minver, Cornwall PL27 6LD
Nearest station: Bodmin Parkway

Attend the Bristol Balloon Fiesta

Europe's largest annual gathering of hot-air balloons has taken place since 1979 at the Ashton Court Estate in Bristol, attracting in excess of 100 balloons and up to 500,000 spectators.

The event takes place over four days in August, with morning and evening balloon ascents, and evening 'nightglows', where the balloons are inflated to glow against the night sky.

Website: www.bristolballoonfiesta.co.uk
Address: Bristol, Avon
Nearest station: Bristol

Drink from the Chalice Well

Bubbling up from the foot of Glastonbury Tor in Somerset, the Chalice Well has long held a mysterious fascination for visitors. Coloured by iron-oxide deposits, which give the water a reddish hue, proponents of both Arthurian and Christian mythology have seized upon the well, and its water is said to have healing properties.

The Chalybeate waters continue to flow from the well ceaselessly and at a steady rate, and with a temperature that never varies, visitors are still able to take a refreshing drink from the well on a hot August afternoon.

Website: www.chalicewell.org.uk
Address: 85-8 Chilkwell Street, Glastonbury, Somerset BA6 8DD
Nearest station: Glastonbury

See the Kettlewell Scarecrows

Every August since 1994, the village of Kettlewell in the Yorkshire Dales has been invaded by an army of scarecrows, designed by villagers for a competition in aid of local charities.

For a fortnight, the band of around 100 scarecrows takes over the village. Covering themes ranging from topical national events, to historical, local and fictional figures and whole sports teams, they can be spotted in gardens, on verges and even on rooftops throughout the village.

Website: www.kettlewellscarecrowfestival.co.uk
Address: Kettlewell Village, Upper Wharfedale, North Yorkshire
Nearest station: Horton-in-Ribblesdale

Sleep in the Treetops

The Mighty Oak Tree Climbing Company specialises in safe climbing experiences in Cornish oak trees, and for those with nerves of steel, they also offer a night with a difference: sleeping in a specially designed hammock at the top of a tree.

The organisers insist the tree-boats – as the hammocks are called – are perfectly safe, and they even serve breakfast in the trees for anyone who wants to savour the experience.

Website: www.mighty-oak.co.uk
Address: St Columb Major, Cornwall
Nearest station: St Columb Road

Escape to Burgh Island

Located on its own private island off the Devon coast, the Art Deco Burgh Island Hotel was built in 1929, a period in which it played host to such glamorous figures as Noël Coward and Agatha Christie.

Though the cost of a night in one of the hotel's themed rooms is beyond the means of most, nonresidents are free to explore the island. Visitors are also welcome for Sunday lunch and evening black-tie dinners, as well as for drinks in the hotel's fourteenth-century pub, the Pilchard Inn, which is known for its curry nights.

Website: www.burghisland.com
Address: Burgh Island Hotel, Bigbury-on-Sea, South Devon TQ7 4BG
Nearest station: Totnes or Plymouth Stations

PICK A WINNER IN THE WORLD HEN RACING CHAMPIONSHIPS

Every year on the first Saturday in August, the Barley Mow in Bonsall, Derbyshire, is transformed into the venue for the World Hen Racing Championships, a highly competitive event that sees prize hens race each other over a fifteen-metre course. The organisers claim their sport can trace its origins back more than a century, to an age when local villages in Derbyshire competed each summer.

While the modern sport has attracted entrants from as far away as Norway, France and Germany, the birds often lack a clear sense of direction and show little interest, resulting in an event that excites the trainers more than it does the hens.

Website: www.world-championship-hen-racing.com
Address: Barley Mow, The Dale, Bonsall, Derbyshire DE4 2AY
Nearest station: Matlock

See Wisbech's Clarkson Memorial

Slavery Remembrance Day on 23 August is a sombre time to reflect on the evils of slavery and give thanks for those who fought for its abolition. The people of Wisbech in Cambridgeshire proudly remember local son Thomas Clarkson, a leading campaigner against the slave trade, in the form of the Clarkson Memorial.

This towering Victorian monument features a statue of Clarkson topped with a sixty-eight-foot canopy, and it stands at the centre of the town in Bridge Street. Built thanks to donations from a local Quaker family and public subscription, the structure was completed in November 1881.

Website: www.historyextra.com/slavery
Address: Bridge Street, Wisbech, Cambridgeshire
Nearest station: Wisbech North; Wisbech East

Walk in Bosworth Field

Though there is some dispute as to the site of the final battle of the Wars of the Roses and whether it was Richard III or William Shakespeare who offered, 'A horse, a horse, my kingdom for a horse!', most historians agree that it took place within a few miles of Ambion Hill, near Sutton Cheney in Leicestershire.

The story of the fifteenth-century battle, which saw the death of Richard III and the subsequent crowning of Henry VII, is now told at Ambion Hill, where the Bosworth Battlefield Heritage Centre puts the battle in context and explains the events that began the Tudor period.

Website: www.bosworthbattlefield.com
Address: Sutton Cheney, Near Market Bosworth, Nuneaton CV13 0AD
Nearest station: Nuneaton and Leicester

Meet the King of Piel Island

At the mouth of the Walney Channel a few miles from Barrow-in-Furness, Piel is a fifty-acre island cut off from the mainland, and home to a ruined fourteenth-century castle and a single pub, the Ship Inn.

   The island is overseen by the King of Piel, a title given to each new landlord of the Ship, who receives an elaborate coronation ceremony. Piel Island can be accessed in summer by boat from neighbouring Roa Island, which is attached to the mainland.

Website: www.pielisland.co.uk
Address: The Ship Inn, Piel Island, Barrow-in-Furness, Lancashire
Nearest station: Barrow-in-Furness

SEARCH FOR CROP CIRCLES FROM THE BARGE INN

As harvest approaches, the rolling fields of the Salisbury Plain are at their most beautiful, covered with waving wheat, barley and other crops. But a mysterious phenomenon has been occurring here since the 1970s, when otherworldly crop circles began appearing in open fields and baffling the locals.

Though two local men – Doug Bower and Dave Chorley – admitted in 1991 to having been the hoaxers behind the creation of many crop circles before that date, and many other pranksters have been caught in the act since, they continue to appear. The Barge Inn in Honey Street, Wiltshire, has become a centre for those who want to see them, either as unexplainable alien creations or simply as beautiful examples of man-made art.

Website: www.the-barge-inn.com
Address: The Barge Inn, Honey Street, Pewsey, Wiltshire SN9 5PS
Nearest station: Pewsey

Visit Eyam Plague Village

In the summer of 1665, an innocent-looking parcel of material from London arrived in the quiet Derbyshire village of Eyam for the village tailor. Within a week, he was dead, and within two months, thirty more villagers had died. Under the direction of the Reverend William Mompesson, the village took the decision to seal itself off from the outside world.

By November 1666, when the plague finally came to an end in Eyam, 260 out of 350 villagers had been struck down by the plague, but the courageous decision of the villagers had helped to protect neighbouring communities. In modern-day Eyam, the final week in August is celebrated as Carnival Week, and alongside a Plague Commemoration Service at the historic church, an annual sheep roast is held in the centre of the village, with the streets garlanded with colourful bunting.

Website: www.eyammuseum.demon.co.uk
Address: : Eyam Museum, Hawkhill Road, Eyam, Derbyshire S32 5QP
Nearest station: Hathersage

See the Site of a Viking Invasion

In August of AD 991, after sacking the town of Ipswich, a huge Viking fleet sailed down the coast and landed at Northey Island in the Blackwater Estuary in Essex, intending to take Maldon. As they waited for the tide to fall, however, they were trapped on the island by the East Saxon forces of Æthelred the Unready, led by Earl Byrhtnoth and his forces.

When the Viking forces were refused payment to leave, Byrhtnoth challenged them to battle, but as the rising tide reduced fighting space on the island, the Vikings were allowed onto the mainland and the Battle of Maldon commenced. It ended in defeat for the Anglo-Saxons. Today, the island is in the care of the National Trust, and can be visited by prior arrangement.

Website: www.nationaltrust.org.uk/northey-island
Address: Northey Island, Maldon CM9 6PP
Nearest station: Maldon

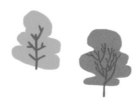

See a Show at Scarborough's Open Air Theatre

Built by Scarborough Corporation in the 1930s in Northstead Manor Gardens, Scarborough's Open Air Theatre is the largest in Europe, with seating for audiences of up to 6,000 people.

After the theatre closed in 1986, its future looked uncertain, but in 2008, planning permission was granted for a major refurbishment, and it reopened in May 2010.

Website: www.scarboroughopenairtheatre.com
Address: Scarborough, North Yorkshire
Nearest station: Scarborough

Watch the Bognor Birdman

Since the 1970s, the Sussex town of Bognor Regis has been the venue for the International Birdman competition, in which competitors vie to see who can fly or jump the furthest from the end of the town's Victorian pier.

The competition attracts 'birdmen' from all over the world to compete in the Leonardo Da Vinci Class, for specially built flying machines, the Kingfisher Class for fun entries, and the elite Condor Class for experienced hang-glider pilots.

Website: www.birdman.org.uk
Address: Bognor Regis, West Sussex
Nearest station: Bognor Regis

Visit England's Largest Vineyard

Denbies Vineyard, on the outskirts of Dorking in the Surrey Hills, is England's largest vineyard, with more than 250 acres of vines. Established in the 1980s in an area that has been known for wine-making since Roman times, the vineyard now produces around 300,000 litres of wine each year.

The area is thought to be one of the best in England for producing wine, similar in climate and soil to the wine-growing regions of Northern France, and wines produced at Denbies have won a number of awards.

Website: www.denbies.co.uk
Address: London Road, Dorking, Surrey RH5 6AA
Nearest station: Dorking

Drink at the World's Smallest Pub

Opened in the summer of 2006, the Signal Box Inn in Cleethorpes claims to be the smallest pub in the world, at just under six square metres.

Originally a signal box beside the Cleethorpes Light Railway, the pub has only four stools and can accommodate up to six customers in its tiny bar.

Website: www.cleethorpescoastlightrailway.co.uk
Address: Lakeside Station, Kings Road, Cleethorpes DN35 0AG
Nearest station: Cleethorpes

WATCH THE BRITISH FIREWORK CHAMPIONSHIPS

Every August since 1997, Plymouth has hosted the National Firework Championships, with spectacular displays from the top fireworks companies watched by tens of thousands of people.

The event brings fireworks experts from around the country to Plymouth, each having an allocated period of time to impress with their displays, with their work painted across the skies over Plymouth Sound.

Website: www.fireworkchampions.co.uk
Address: The Hoe, Plymouth, Devon PL1 2LR
Nearest station: Plymouth

Notes

....

....

....

....

....

....

....

....

September

While September usually begins with hot summery days, by the end of the month summer is in its death throes, with the first bite of autumn seeing leaves begin to change colour and the ushering in of conker season.

The harvest season traditionally ends at Michaelmas on 29 September. This was also the final day of the fishing season, the day the winter night curfew began, and the day after which blackberries should not be picked. Harvest festivals begin around the country, usually coinciding with the Harvest Moon at the end of the month, and the final festivals mark the end of summer weather, with the start of the long Sussex bonfire season and the lengthening of the evenings.

Admire the Art of Newlyn Gallery

Opened in 1895, in Newlyn, near Penzance, Newlyn Art Gallery was established to exhibit the art of the Newlyn School, a group of Victorian artists who based themselves in the small fishing village in order to paint *en plein air*, observing the unique light and scenery of West Cornwall.

The gallery is still going strong, and, following redevelopments in 2007, has been extended with the inevitable addition of an attractive café with panoramic sea views.

Website: www.newlynartgallery.co.uk
Address: New Road, Newlyn, Penzance, Cornwall TR18 5PZ
Nearest station: Penzance

Take the Kielder Forest Drive

A twelve-mile drive passing through forest and high moorland between Redesdale and Kielder Water, the Kielder Forest Drive is about as remote as it is possible to get in England.

The single-track unsurfaced road peaks at over 1,500 feet at Blakehope Nick, where it passes beneath the poetically named Oh Me Edge, before descending through the forest towards Kielder Castle, where vehicles are requested to pay a small toll to help with maintenance.

Website: www.visitkielder.com
Address: Kielder, Hexham, Northumberland NE48 1ER
Nearest station: Hexham

Visit Lawrence of Arabia's Hut in the Woods

Following the desert campaigns that made him famous, T E Lawrence returned to England and joined the Royal Tank Corps. He was stationed at Bovington Camp, and it was during this time he rented Clouds Hill, a tiny cottage in the woods that was owned by his relations, the Frampton family.

Lawrence bought Clouds Hill two years later and owned it until 1935 when, aged forty-six and only a short while after leaving military service, he died following a motorcycle accident close to the cottage. He is buried in the churchyard at St Nicholas Church in nearby Moreton, and Clouds Hill is maintained as a museum of his life.

Website: www.nationaltrust.org.uk/clouds-hill
Address: Wareham, Dorset BH20 7NQ
Nearest station: Wareham

Watch the Birds at Gilbraltar Point

Not quite as exotic as its Iberian cousin, Gibraltar Point is a nature reserve at the northern end of the Wash in Lincolnshire, covering over 1,000 acres of sand, mud, dunes, saltmarshes and freshwater lakes.

Despite its bleak appearance, the area is a paradise for birds, and is managed by the Lincolnshire Wildlife Trust to ensure it remains so.

Website: www.lincstrust.org.uk/reserves/gib
Address: Gibraltar Road, Skegness PE24 4SU
Nearest station: Skegness

SEEK INSPIRATION FROM NEWTON'S APPLE TREE

During the mid-1660s, as the plague ravaged towns and cities around the country, Isaac Newton left Cambridge and retreated to his childhood home at Woolsthorpe Manor in Lincolnshire. There he began his annus mirabilis, a miraculous year during which many of his most celebrated theories were developed.

Though other trees also lay claim to being the one from which Newton observed an apple falling to the ground, helping him to develop his theory of gravity, many believe that it was while musing in the grounds at Woolsthorpe that Newton had his eureka moment, and the tree still growing in the garden is celebrated as the original.

Website: www.nationaltrust.org.uk/woolsthorpe-manor
Address: Water Lane, Woolsthorpe by Colsterworth, Grantham, Lincolnshire NG33 5PD
Nearest station: Grantham

ENTER THE WORLD BLACK PUDDING THROWING CHAMPIONSHIPS

For one weekend each September, the Victorian mill town of Ramsbottom in Lancashire becomes the international centre for the sport of Black Pudding Throwing, with participants gathering outside the Royal Oak in Bridge Street to attempt to dislodge a stack of Yorkshire Puddings from a twenty-foot-tall ledge by hitting it with black puddings.

Throwers make the unlikely claim that their contest owes its creation to a battle of the Wars of the Roses – a series of conflicts between the Yorkists and Lancastrians – when the two sides ran out of ammunition near Ramsbottom and were forced to throw food at each other.

Website: www.calendarcustoms.com/articles/world-black-pudding-throwing-championships
Address: Outside the Royal Oak Pub, 39 Bridge Street, Ramsbottom, Bury BL0 9AD
Nearest station: Bolton

Visit Grime's Graves

A Neolithic flint mine in the heart of Breckland Heath in North Suffolk, Grime's Graves are among the oldest industrial sites in Europe, dug over 5,000 years ago by the hands of Prehistoric Man. Those working in the mines – which were in use until the Early Bronze Age – used picks made from deer antlers to dig shafts up to forty feet deep into the chalk.

The area was named Grime's Graves by the Anglo-Saxons due to its pockmarked appearance. The mines were rediscovered during Victorian excavation work, and are now open to the public.

Website: www.brandonsuffolk.com/grimes-graves.asp
Address: Grimes Graves, Lynford, Norfolk, IP26 5DE
Nearest station: Brandon

Drive over Hardknott Pass

Often cited as the steepest road in England, Hardknott Pass is a single-track road cutting between the high peaks of the Lake District, passing from Eskdale to the Duddon Valley. In places, the road achieves a gradient of 1 in 3, as its hairpin bends wind their way down the hillside, with signs warning drivers not to attempt it in large vehicles or wintry conditions.

The pass offers fantastic views over surrounding countryside, and a Roman fort, perched at the bottom of the steepest section, is an excellent vantage point to take in the snaking route.

Website: www.rural-roads.co.uk/lakes/wrynose4.shtml
Address: Near Eskdale, Cumbria
Nearest station: Ravenglass

Walk in Flodden Field

On the morning of 9 September 1513, in miserable weather, the Scottish and English armies faced each other at Flodden Field near the village of Branxton, Northumberland, in the largest battle ever fought between the two kingdoms.

Just a few hours later, more than 10,000 men lay dead, including James IV of Scotland, the last Scottish monarch to die in battle. The result was a decisive victory for the English, with many of the most important members of the Scottish nobility killed alongside their king. The Flodden Monument on Piper's Hill remembers the dead of both nations.

Website: www.flodden.net/
Address: Branxton Villa, Branxton, Northumberland, TD12 4SW
Nearest station: Berwick-upon-Tweed

Hire a Vintage Sports Car

Known for the distinctive driving experience it offers, the Caterham Seven is the successor to the Lotus Seven, a super-lightweight car designed by Lotus founder Colin Chapman and built by the company until the 1970s.

Today, the Seven is produced by Caterham Cars in Surrey. Those wanting to experience the unique performance and handling of these open-top cars but unable to afford such an impractical toy can rent them by the day from Blue Sky at Cragg Hall Farm in Galgate near Lancaster.

Website: www.blueskycaterham.co.uk
Address: Blue Sky Caterham Hire LLP, Cragg Hall Farm, Galgate, Lancaster LA2 0HN
Nearest station: Galgate

Explore the Pitt Rivers Museum

A fascinating museum operated by the University of Oxford, the Pitt Rivers Museum displays treasures from its vast collection of anthropology and world archaeology in its multi-layered hall.

Founded in 1884, and based on the collection of archaeologist and ethnologist General Pitt Rivers, the museum houses hundreds of dark and eerie cases displaying some half a million objects, including mummies, shrunken heads, Hawaiian feather cloaks and weapons used in tribal warfare.

Website: www.prm.ox.ac.uk
Address: South Parks Road, Oxford OX1 3PP
Nearest station: Oxford

Explore Salt's Mill

The huge former textile mill at Saltaire, near Shipley in West Yorkshire, built in 1853 by Victorian industrialist Sir Titus Salt, was once the largest factory in the world, employing 3,000 people. After closing in the 1980s, the mill was purchased by Jonathan Silver, an acquaintance of David Hockney, and transformed into Salt's Mill (*above*), home to gallery and commercial spaces, including the 1853 Gallery, which now displays one of the largest collections of David Hockney's art.

The surrounding neighbourhood is a fascinating example of the scale of Victorian industry, with the model village of workers' churches, schools and houses declared a UNESCO World Heritage Site in 2001. In mid-September, the area is the venue for the annual Saltaire Arts Festival.

Website: www.saltsmill.org.uk
Address: Victoria Road, Shipley, Saltaire, West Yorkshire BD18 3LA
Nearest station: Shipley

Visit Brantwood

In 1871, the celebrated Victorian radical, writer, art critic, poet and watercolour painter, John Ruskin, moved to Brantwood, a beautiful house in the Lake District, set within 250 acres of woodland. Previously owned by the poet Gerald Massey, the house was to become Ruskin's home until his death in 1900, and he quickly set about reshaping it to meet his needs.

Ruskin filled Brantwood with art and books and added a turret to his bedroom, to allow him to make the most of the spectacular views, while the garden became a living laboratory in which he undertook experiments in land management and horticulture. Today, the house is opened to the public by a charitable trust, in memory of the great man.

Website: www.brantwood.org.uk
Address: Brantwood, Coniston, Cumbria LA21 8AD
Nearest station: Windermere; Ulverston

Climb to Ilfracombe's Lighthouse Chapel

A pretty little building above Ilfracombe Harbour, St Nicholas' Chapel dates from 1321. Since the Middle Ages, a light has burned in its turret to guide shipping into the harbour.

After it ceased to be a chapel in the sixteenth century, the building variously became a home, a reading room and even a laundry. Today, it is maintained by the local Rotary Club, with an interesting display about its history and relationship with the town.

Website: www.visitilfracombe.co.uk
Address: Ilfracombe Harbour, Ilfracombe, Devon EX34 9EQ
Nearest station: Barnstaple

Climb Scafell Pike

A number of paths wind their way up England's highest mountain, Scafell Pike in the Lake District, with the most well-trodden route taking walkers from Wasdale Head to the top. Some consider the walk from Seathwaite Farm in Borrowdale to be the best route, while other popular routes arrive at the summit from Langdale and Eskdale.

Many of those who prefer the Wasdale Head route like to end their descent at the Wasdale Head Inn, known as the birthplace of British climbing because of its connections to the earliest Victorian pioneers, who came here to enjoy the Cumbrian scenery.

Website: www.scafellpike.org.uk
Address: Lake District National Park, Cumbria
Nearest station: Penrith

See the Birthplace of D H Lawrence

David Herbert Lawrence was born on 11 September 1885, in the coal-mining town of Eastwood, Nottinghamshire.

The modest house in which Lawrence was born – 8a Victoria Street – is now a museum of his life and the lives of others who lived in the area. Nearby Durban House, where Lawrence used to collect his father's mining wages, is now the D H Lawrence Heritage Centre, which contains an exhibition on his life.

Website: www.nottingham.ac.uk/dhlheritage/
Address: 8a Victoria Street, Eastwood, Notts., NG16 3SA
Nearest station: Langley Mill

Watch for Whales off Whitby

The North Yorkshire town of Whitby has a long history as a whaling port, an industry that saw ships frequently sailing as far as Greenland and the Arctic Circle during the eighteenth and nineteenth centuries. The town's whaling history is commemorated by the Whitby Whalebone Arch – an arch made from the jawbone of a whale.

However, Whitby's whales are not all in the past: in late summer, early autumn, whales are seen off the coast of the town, with Whitby Coastal Cruises offering whale-watching trips from the harbour.

Website: www.whitbycoastalcruises.co.uk/
Address: The Brewery Steps, Lower Harbour, Whitby, YO21 3PR
Nearest station: Whitby

ATTEND THE ANNUAL KENDAL TORCHLIGHT CARNIVAL

Since the 1970s, the Cumbrian town of Kendal has been celebrating the beginning of autumn with a Torchlight Carnival, seeing floats, dancers, bands and locals form a procession through the streets at night. Volunteers and community organisations decorate their tractors, engines, bicycles and other vehicles for the parade.

Claiming to draw inspiration from a time when those living in outlying Lakeland villages would come to Kendal to stock up on provisions before a long hard winter, the carnival is still a highlight of the local calendar.

Website: www.kendaltorchlightcarnival.co.uk
Address: Kendal, Cumbria
Nearest station: Kendal

Seek Peace at the Kadampa Temple

Conishead Priory, on the Cumbrian coast near Ulverston, has had an interesting life. Originally the site of a twelfth-century Augustinian priory, and later a nineteenth-century Gothic-revival country house, by the 1930s it had been acquired by the Durham Miners' Welfare Committee as a convalescence home for injured miners.

Today, the estate has found a new purpose as an international college for Buddhist studies, and the Kadampa Temple for World Peace now sits in the grounds, housing the largest bronze statue of Buddha ever cast in the West. The seventy-acre estate on the shores of Morecambe Bay is open to the public most of the time, offering panoramic views out across the bay towards Chapel Island.

Website: www.nkt-kmc-manjushri.org
Address: Kadampa Temple, Conishead Priory, Ulverston LA12 9QQ
Nearest station: Ulverston

Visit the Samuel Johnson Birthplace Museum and Bookshop

The great eighteenth-century writer, lexicographer and man of letters, Dr Samuel Johnson, was born in an imposing house on Lichfield's Market Square. Built in 1707 by Johnson's bookseller father, Michael, it served as both a home and bookshop. Dr Johnson lived in the house for his first twenty-seven years and returned frequently throughout his lifetime.

Since 1901, the Grade I-listed building has been home to the Samuel Johnson Birthplace Museum and Bookshop, offering a window onto the life of one of the greatest men of his time, and also providing the headquarters of the Johnson Society.

Website: www.samueljohnsonbirthplace.org.uk
Address: Breadmarket Street, Lichfield, Staffordshire WS13 6LG
Nearest station: Lichfield

CLIMB MAM TOR

A popular hill in the Peak District, topped with an Iron Age hill fort, Mam Tor – which is believed to translate as 'Mother Hill' – stands 1,696 feet high at the head of the Hope Valley.

From the top, where the outline of the hill fort's remains are still visible, there are excellent views down into Edale and the Hope Valley, where trains can be seen working their way along the Hope Valley Line.

Website: peakdistrict.nationaltrust.org.uk/mam-tor
Address: Castleton, Peak District, Derbyshire
Nearest station: Hope (Derbyshire)

Go Fishing at the Arundell Arms

An historic hotel in the village of Lifton, on the border between Devon and Cornwall, the Arundell Arms Hotel is known for its fishing school, which offers a range of fishing in the area's wild rivers.

The hotel has fishing rights for stretches of seven rivers, including the Tamar, which forms the border between Devon and Cornwall, and six other tributaries. The hotel offers fishing for many different abilities and in September both brown trout and salmon are in season.

Website: www.arundellarms.com
Address: 1 Fore Street, Lifton, Devon PL16 0AA
Nearest station: Exeter

Take Tea at Bettys

The first Bettys Tea Rooms were opened in Harrogate in 1919, by a Swiss confectioner named Frederick Belmont, who, after misplacing his travel directions from London, found himself in the Bradford area, discovered it reminded him of Switzerland, and decided to set up his own business.

Since then, Bettys has gone from strength to strength, and now has branches across Yorkshire, but the most famous is still the Tea Rooms in Harrogate, which offers customers a choice of hundreds of breads, cakes and chocolates, and fifty different teas and coffees.

Website: www.bettys.co.uk
Address: 1 Parliament St, Harrogate, North Yorkshire HG1 2QU
Nearest station: Harrogate

Parade with the Uckfield Bonfire Society

The annual Uckfield Carnival dates back to 1827, when the first event was organised by local shopkeepers in the Sussex town. It now takes place on the first Saturday in September.

The popular event marks the start of the annual Sussex Bonfire season, which runs until early November, with the Uckfield Bonfire Society leading the festivities before spending the autumn visiting other towns to participate in their bonfire celebrations.

Website: www.uckfieldcarnival.co.uk
Address: Uckfield, East Sussex
Nearest station: Uckfield

Cross the Humber Bridge

Still known in political circles as 'the biggest election bribe in history', the Humber Bridge cost £151 million to construct, a figure to which Labour Transport Secretary Barbara Castle affirmed her commitment during a fierce 1966 by-election battle.

The bridge was finally opened in 1981, and for more than fifteen years was the longest single-span bridge in the world. Today, it carries more than 6 million vehicles a year on a journey of nearly a mile and a half across the Humber Estuary.

Website: www.humberbridge.co.uk
Address: Near Kingston-upon-Hull
Nearest station: Hull

Eat in a Bookshop in Hastings Old Town

On an atmospheric ambling street in Hastings Old Town, the Boulevard Bookshop and Thai Café offers diners a chance to eat at a table among the shelves of a genuine second-hand bookshop.

Opened in March 2009, by owners June and Graham, the shop is a normal bookshop during working hours, but in the evenings tables are erected and guests are then free to browse while their food is prepared.

Website: www.thaicafeandbookshop.com
Address: 32 George Street, Hastings, East Sussex TN34 3EA
Nearest station: Hastings

Have Kippers at Craster

The small fishing village of Craster in Northumberland has long been known for its kippers, and at L. Robson & Sons, the fish are still cured in original smokehouses, as they have been for over 130 years.

Though smoked fish has been eaten for centuries, legend has it that the modern kipper was invented by accident in 1843 at Seahouses, just up the coast, when a split herring was left in a shed in which a fire had been left smouldering overnight.

Website: www.kipper.co.uk
Address: L. Robson & Sons, Haven Hill, Craster, Alnwick, Northumberland NE66 3TR
Nearest station: Alnmouth

Attend Stroud Farmers' Market

One of Britain's best farmers' markets, Stroud specialises in food and drink from local producers and attracts visitors from around the country. The town sits at the heart of five valleys, and its market takes place every Saturday until 2 p.m., with around sixty stalls a week.

The town has always had a tradition of nonconformity and was at the forefront of the organic food movement – Woodruffs Café, just a short walk away, claims to be Britain's first wholly organic café – so a strong selection of organic produce is usually found at the market.

Website: www.fresh-n-local.co.uk/markets/stroud
Address: Cornhill Market Place, Stroud, Gloucestershire
Nearest station: Gloucester

Visit the Tate St Ives

While many Londoners think that the only Tate galleries are in Bankside and Pimlico, the people of St Ives and Liverpool have their own versions, offering the same high-quality art exhibitions in places with strong artistic pedigrees.

Designed by architects Evans and Shalev, on the site of a former gas works, the Tate St Ives is found on the town's Porthmeor Beach. Opened in 1993, it offers a selection of exhibitions, including regular shows of art inspired by the seaside town.

Website: www.tate.org.uk/visit/tate-st-ives
Address: Porthmeor Hill, St Ives, Cornwall TR26 1TG
Nearest station: St Ives

Go Gurning at Egremont Crab Fair

One of the oldest fairs in the world, the annual Crab Fair in the Cumbrian town of Egremont has been held since 1267, taking its name not from crustaceans but from crab apples, which were traditionally given away at the fair by the Lord of Egremont.

Best known as the home of the World Gurning Championship – a competition to pull the most distorted facial expression – the fair also features a greasy-pole-climbing competition and other unusual entertainments.

Website: www.egremontcrabfair.com
Address: Egremont, Cumbria
Nearest station: Breystones

October

This is a month marked by autumn colours, misty days and the first winter birds, as farmers begin ploughing the fields for next year's crops. With the harvest newly gathered, and preparations for winter being made, October was once a time for fairs, offering a last chance to do trade in livestock and produce before the winter.

October is still a time of relative plenty, and even at the end of the month, events such as Halloween or Punkie Night maintain harvest associations, with apple bobbing and vegetable lanterns. It also used to be a time for battling, and the battles of Hastings, Edgehill, Trafalgar and Agincourt all took place during a month that marked the end of the traditional spring-to-autumn fighting season.

Eat One of Sally Lunn's Buns

According to tales told by Marie Byng-Johnson, the former owner of Sally Lunn's house, a young French Huguenot refugee named Sally Lunn arrived in Bath in the late seventeenth century. She took work at a bakery at what is now 4 North Parade Passage, baking delicate and light 'buns' at the bakery that were the first of their kind in pre-Georgian Bath.

Today, the house – one of the oldest in Bath – is preserved, along with its kitchen, as a café and living museum, including the secret cupboard in which Byng-Johnson claimed to have found Lunn's original recipes. Whether Sally Lunn really existed is open to speculation, but her story continues to enchant visitors, as it has for generations.

Website: www.sallylunns.co.uk
Address: Sally Lunns House, 4 North Parade Passage Bath, BA1 1NX
Nearest station: Bath

Visit Charleston Farmhouse

In October 1916, the artist Vanessa Bell moved into Charleston Farmhouse in East Sussex with her unconventional household, which included her two children, fellow artist and occasional lover, Duncan Grant, and his then lover, David Garnett. Bell was to maintain her connection with Charleston until her death in 1961, as the house became the country home of the Bloomsbury Group, which included her sister, Virginia Woolf, the economist, John Maynard Keynes, and various writers, painters and intellectuals such as E M Forster, Lytton Strachey and Roger Fry.

Today, Charleston is preserved by the Charleston Trust, which maintains the house and gardens as they would have looked when the Bloomsbury Group came here, complete with fabrics and ceramics from the Group's Omega Workshops in London's Fitzroy Square. Visitors get the chance to step into the studio, added to the house in 1925 in what had previously been a chicken run.

Website: www.charleston.org.uk
Address: Charleston, Firle, Lewes, East Sussex BN8 6LL
Nearest station: Lewes

VISIT THE PEOPLE'S HISTORY MUSEUM

Tracing its origins from the Trade Union, Labour and Co-operative History Society, Manchester's People's History Museum started in the 1960s as a small collection exhibited at Limehouse Town Hall in London between 1975 and 1986. The museum offers an unrivalled collection of artefacts and exhibits on social history, unionism and struggle around the country, with an occasional particular focus on Manchester.

The museum came to Manchester thanks to funding offers from local authorities, and opened in 1990 on Princess Street. After a refurbishment between 2007 and 2010, it reopened on the left bank of the River Irwell, where it is free to visit daily.

Website: www.phm.org.uk
Address: People's History Museum, Left Bank, Manchester, Lancashire M3 3ER
Nearest station: Manchester Piccadilly

Drink at the Pandora Inn

A beautiful thatched pub at the end of a long Cornish lane, the Pandora Inn sits beside sleepy Restronguet Creek between Falmouth and Truro. The building was a farmhouse until the thirteenth century, when it became a pub.

Though it was the victim of a horrific fire in 2011, the pub has now fully recovered and the interior has been restored using traditional building methods and correct materials, as dictated by its Grade II listing.

Website: www.pandorainn.com
Address: Pandora Inn, Restronguet Hill, Falmouth, Cornwall TR11 5ST
Nearest station: Perranwell; Falmouth Docks

Cross Otterburn Ranges

The Ministry of Defence owns nearly a quarter of Northumberland National Park, and when it is not in use for military training, anyone is free to access the land, as long as they stick to marked paths and lanes and avoid military debris.

As such, the Otterburn Ranges offer 60,000 acres of remote upland, with heather moorland and birch woodland as far as the eye can see. There are hundreds of miles of tranquil surfaced lanes and bridleways, with the potential for some breath taking rides and walks in an area with a visible history: from Roman forts and marching camps to ancient borderland Bastle houses and First World War training trenches.

Website: www.northumberlandnationalpark.org.uk
Address: Eastburn, South Park, Hexham, Northumberland, NE46 1BS
Nearest station: Hexham

Watch the Matlock Bath Illuminations

For more than a century, the Derbyshire village of Matlock Bath has been lighting up its stretch of the River Derwent each autumn, with a procession of illuminated and decorated boats.

The first such event was held in 1897, to celebrate the Diamond Jubilee of Queen Victoria. Nowadays, the Matlock Bath illuminations take place on weekends each October (and late September), led by a candle-lit boat and accompanied by firework displays on Saturday evenings to coincide with the procession.

Website: www.derbyshiredales.gov.uk
Address: Derwent Gardens, Matlock, Derbyshire DE4 3LX
Nearest station: Matlock Bath

See the Zetland Lifeboat

On 7 October 1802, the Zetland Lifeboat – built by pioneering South Shields lifeboat builder Henry Greathead – arrived at Redcar on the North Sea coast and began a seventy-eight-year career, which would see her save more than 500 lives

Today, over 200 years later, the Zetland is the oldest surviving lifeboat in the world and can still be seen in Redcar, where its story is told in a small museum, funded by the RNLI.

Website: http://rnli.org/aboutus/historyandheritage/museums/Pages/Zetland-Museum.aspx
Address: The Esplanade, Redcar, Cleveland, TS10 3AH
Nearest station: Redcar Central; Redcar East

See the Autumn Colours at Westonbirt Arboretum

Started in the mid-1800s, by Victorian landowner Robert Holford, Westonbirt Arboretum is a collection of some 16,000 trees featuring 2,500 different species from countries all over the world, including Britain, China, North America, Japan and Chile.

The Arboretum offers a spectacular display of colour in autumn, covering 600 acres, and with seventeen miles of pathways through the trees. It has been run by the Forestry Commission since 1956, and attracts around 350,000 visitors a year.

Website: www.forestry.gov.uk/westonbirt
Address: Westonbirt, Tetbury, Gloucestershire, GL8 8QS
Nearest station: Kemble

Attend the Nottingham Goose Fair

For more than seven centuries, the people of Nottingham have gathered for the autumnal Goose Fair. It is an event that began as a sale of thousands of geese, driven from the Lincolnshire Fens and sold to provide the basis for a traditional Michaelmas dinner. The fair is an important local tradition, and has survived cancellations in years of plague and during the two World Wars, even overcoming riots about the price of cheese in 1764.

Though the fair was originally held in Nottingham's Old Market Square in late September, it moved to early October in the eighteenth century, following the adoption of the Gregorian calendar. The fair has been held at the Forest Recreation Ground since the late 1920s, and the modern visitor is more likely to find scores of funfair rides than geese and cheese salesmen.

Website: www.experiencenottinghamshire.com
Address: Gregory Boulevard, Nottingham, Nottinghamshire, NG7 6JP
Nearest station: Nottingham

DINE IN TITANIC LUXURY AT THE WHITE SWAN

The White Swan Hotel, in the Northumberland town of Alnwick, hides a dining room of titanic proportions – in this case quite literally. The fixtures and fittings in the dining room were taken directly from the Titanic's sister ship, the **RMS** *Olympic*, which was launched in the same year and designed in exactly the same luxurious style.

When the *Olympic* was broken up in the 1930s, the fittings and artworks were auctioned and acquired by a former owner of the hotel, who reconstructed them here. The dining room contains the original panelling, mirrors, ceiling and stained-glass windows from the days when the *Olympic* still conducted voyages around the world.

Website: www.classiclodges.co.uk/The_White_Swan_Hotel_Alnwick
Address: The White Swan, Bondgate Within, Alnwick, Northumberland, NE66 1TD
Nearest station: Alnmouth

Visit Kilpeck Church

The tiny sandstone church of St Mary and St David at Kilpeck, Herefordshire, is noted for its Norman carvings depicting serpents, angels, a green man, a Sheela-na Gig and a menagerie of beasts.

The church, which is thought to contain remnants of its earlier Saxon foundations, is entered through a spectacular Norman arch. The St David in its name is most likely a local Celtic saint rather than the celebrated Welsh one, while the name of the village itself is thought to derive from Pedic, a local early-Christian hermit.

Website: www.sacred-destinations.com/england/kilpeck-church.htm
Address: St Mary and St David in Kilpeck, Herefordshire HR2 9DN
Nearest station: Hereford

Drink in England's Last Parlour Bar

Run for seventy-four years by landlady Flossie Lane, until she died in 2009, the Sun Inn, in the Herefordshire village of Leintwardine, is an original parlour bar where ales were served from barrels on the kitchen floor and drunk by regulars in Flossie's living room.

Though some concession has been made to the twenty-first century in the form of a modern extension, Flossie's original living room is preserved as it was when she passed away, giving drinkers an insight into how a rural Victorian beerhouse would have looked.

Website: www.suninn-leintwardine.co.uk
Address: The Sun Inn, Rosemary Lane, Leintwardine, Herts., SY7 0LP
Nearest station: Bucknell

Take to the Air by Catapult

The gliders of the Long Mynd in Shropshire are a fearless bunch. In high winds their planes are flung into the air off the sides of ridges by a rather long bungee rope pulled by a handful of volunteers. This is one of the few places in the world where this technique is used.

One of the oldest clubs in the country, the Midland Gliding Club has been flying from the Long Mynd since the 1930s, and continues to offer glider pilots and potential pilots a way to get airborne via training courses, trial lessons and regular recreational flying.

Website: www.longmynd.com
Address: Midland Gliding Club, Long Mynd, Shropshire SY6 6TA
Nearest station: Church Stretton

Observe the New Forest Deer Rut

From late September until the end of October, the New Forest is home to one of the country's greatest natural spectacles, as the annual red deer rut sees Britain's largest land mammals enter their annual mating period.

The rut sees stags compete for hinds (female deer) by roaring and grunting, parallel walking with an opponent, and fighting head to head with their antlers. The best time to view this extraordinary event is early morning and evening, but take care not to get too close to stags.

Website: www.new-forest-national-park.com
Address: Bolderwood Arboretum Ornamental Dr, Minstead SO43 7GQ
Nearest station: Brockenhurst

Fly a Kite in the Malvern Hills

A windy October day makes for especially good kite-flying in the Malvern Hills, an eight-mile ridge that runs south from the spa town of Great Malvern.

The hills are made from ancient igneous rocks, so hard that they have resisted erosion over millions of years, and offer steep slopes producing good steady winds. The twin Herefordshire and Worcestershire Beacons also offer good spots.

Website: www.malvernhills.org.uk
Address: Malvern Hills, Worcestershire
Nearest station: Great Malvern; Malvern Link

Walk the Walls of York

Some of the most complete in England, York's city walls still almost encircle the city. Based on an original network of Roman walls, those in place today were largely constructed between the twelfth and fourteenth centuries.

The best views are found by walking the tops of the walls, which offer interesting perspectives on York Minster, the River Ouse and other landmarks. The walls, though broken, feature four grand gatehouses, at Bootham Bar, Micklegate Bar, Monk Bar and Walmgate Bar, which once welcomed people into the city. Both Micklegate Bar and Monk Bar have been converted into museums, which are open to the public.

Website: http://micklegatebar.com/city-walls/
Address: City of York
Nearest station: York

Drink at the Fleece Inn

Originally constructed in the fifteenth century as a longhouse, the Fleece Inn is a Worcestershire institution, acting as the venue for many local traditions, including an annual Asparagus Festival in May and an Apple and Ale Festival in October.

Amazingly, the inn remained in the same family until 1977, when elderly owner Lola Taplin passed away peacefully in front of the fire in the snug. She left it to the National Trust, making the Fleece Inn the Trust's first pub. Following a fire in 2004, it underwent extensive renovation, but is now back on original form.

Website: http://www.thefleeceinn.co.uk/
Address: The Fleece Inn, The Cross Bretforton Nr Evesham WR11 7JE
Nearest station: Honeybourne; Evesham

Discover Ted Hughes's Mytholmroyd

The poet Ted Hughes grew up in Mytholmroyd, an industrial village near Hebden Bridge in Yorkshire. Born at 1 Aspinall Street, he lived here until his family moved to South Yorkshire.

Despite only having lived in the village for a relatively short period, Hughes retained strong memories of the fields, woods and moors around Mytholmroyd and drew on them in later poetry. The Elmet Trust, which promotes interest in the life and works of Ted Hughes, holds an annual Ted Hughes Festival in the village each October.

Website: www.theelmettrust.co.uk/mytholmroyd/birthplace.htm
Address: Mytholmroyd, Hebden Bridge
Nearest station: Mytholmroyd

LISTEN FOR THE LOST IN THE DARK PEAL

Each 7 October, the bells of St Mary's Church at Twyford in Hampshire ring out in the morning and evening to guide the lost to church. The tradition began following a particularly dark night on this date in 1754, when William Davis became lost while out riding his horse in the Hampshire countryside.

Just as he was about to ride over a cliff into a deep quarry, Davis heard the bells of St Mary's and realised his mistake. He was so grateful that he left a pound for each year the bellringers made sure a peal of bells rang out on the date of his near-calamity. Although the money ran out long ago, the tradition still continues.

Website: www.stmarytwyford.fsnet.co.uk
Address: St Mary the Virgin, Church Lane, Twyford, Hampshire, SO21 1NT
Nearest station: Twyford

Climb to the Top of Malham Cove

A stunning eighty-metre carboniferous limestone cliff, formed from meltwater after the last Ice Age, Malham Cove looms above the village of Malham in the Yorkshire Dales. Four hundred stone steps lead to the top, where you can appreciate stunning views and a natural limestone pavement fissured and fretted by rainwater channels.

The rock formation is spectacular and was painted by Turner in 1810, during a tour of Yorkshire, and the place has also inspired the likes of William Wordsworth, John Ruskin, Charles Kingsley and J R R Tolkien. The latter is said to have based the Helm's Deep fortress in his Middle-Earth novels on his experiences here. The view from the top is as uplifting as it has ever been.

Website: www.malhamdale.com/cove.htm
Address: Cove Road, Malham
Nearest station: Gargrave; Skipton

Walk Hastings Battlefield

The death of Edward the Confessor in January 1066 began one of the most turbulent periods in England's history, which finally came to a head in a notorious skirmish in a field six miles outside Hastings on 14 October: the Battle of Hastings.

The battle – which is often re-enacted in October – was the beginning of the Norman invasion, which altered the course of the country's history. At the site of the battle – now the Sussex village of Battle – visitors can take a tour of the battlefield and see the spot where King Harold was killed. They can also explore the ruins of an abbey built by the Normans after the Pope ordered them to do penance for killing so many people in the invasion.

Website: www.english-heritage.org.uk
Address: High Street, Battle, East Sussex, TN33 0AD
Nearest station: Battle

Find Sanctuary at the Sailors' Reading Room

A place for local sailors to rest and recuperate, the Sailors' Reading Room (*above*) in Southwold, Suffolk, was built in 1864 in memory of Captain Rayley, a Naval Officer at the time of the Battle of Trafalgar. Today, it is a registered charity and, as well as being a place for local fishermen and lifeboatmen to gather, it also forms a small museum, open to the public on the seafront of this attractive seaside town.

Alongside exhibits on maritime and local history, the Reading Room holds a collection of pictures and seascapes, as well as portraits of local fishermen, model ships and ship figureheads, cared for by the sailors who come here to read the papers and discuss the issues of the day.

Website: http://suffolkmuseums.org
Address: East Cliff, Southwold, Suffolk, IP18 6EL
Nearest station: Darsham; Halesworth

Climb the Tyndale Monument

High on the hill above North Nibley in Gloucestershire, a 111-foot stone tower (*above*) commemorates William Tyndale, who produced one of the first English translations of the Bible. At a time of strict Catholicism, Tyndale's translations were condemned in England, and he was eventually put to death by strangulation and burning at the stake.

The monument to Tyndale's death, which is usually commemorated on 6 October, was erected in 1886, and is usually open for visitors to climb – if not, the key is available from the village shop.

Website: www.britishlistedbuildings.co.uk
Address: Nibley Knoll summit, North Nibley, Gloucestershire, England
Nearest station: Cam & Dursley; Stroud

FIND THE GRAVE OF A SIKH MAHARAJAH

A leafy graveyard in the small Suffolk village of Elveden marks the final resting place of Duleep Singh, the last Maharajah of the Sikh Empire, and former ruler of the Punjab in Northern India. As a result of the Second Anglo-Sikh War of the late 1840s, and the subsequent annexation of the Punjab, the young Maharajah lost power and came under the control of the British.

Exiled to England at the age of fifteen, Duleep Singh spent many years living as a country squire at Elveden Hall, eventually dying at a hotel in Paris in October 1893. He was buried at the churchyard alongside his wife and son and is commemorated with a bronze statue at Button Island in nearby Thetford.

Website: www.asht.info/trail/288/elveden-parish-church.html
Address: St Andrew & St Patrick Parish Church, Elveden, Suffolk
Nearest station: Thetford; Brandon

Walk the Decks of HMS *Victory*

In October, HMS *Victory* marks one of the most important anniversaries in the Navy calendar, with the ship specially dressed for Trafalgar Day. Though she took part in a number of campaigns, Nelson's flagship is by far best known for her role in the Battle of Trafalgar, in October 1805, a battle in which the great Admiral was shot and killed while aboard.

Despite no longer spending time at sea, having been retired from official service in 1812 and held in dry dock since 1922, HMS *Victory* is still the flagship of the First Sea Lord and used for ceremonial purposes, making it the oldest commissioned warship in the world.

Website: www.hms-victory.com
Address: Portsmouth Historic Dockyard Visitors Centre Hampshire
PO1 3NH
Nearest station: Portsmouth Harbour

Remember Grace Darling

In the early hours of 7 September 1838, lighthouse keeper's daughter Grace Darling looked out from her upstairs window at Longstone Lighthouse in Northumberland's Farne Islands to see a wreck foundering close to the nearby island, and made out the shape of a few survivors clinging to the rocks.

The SS *Forfarshire* had hit the jagged coast and action was needed to save the survivors. With the storm still raging, a lifeboat was unable to put out from Seahouses, and it was up to Grace and her father to rescue the survivors in an open boat. Afterwards, Grace was celebrated as a national hero until her death in 1842 at the age of twenty-six. An RNLI museum in Bamburgh, established in 1938, commemorates her.

Website: www.trinityhouse.co.uk/lighthouses/lighthouse_list/
longstone.html
Address: Longstone Rock, Bamburgh, Berwick-upon-Tweed
Nearest station: Chathill; Alnmouth

Take a Stroll on Crosby Beach

A three-mile stretch of sand north of the Port of Liverpool, Crosby Beach has become famous among art-lovers as the home of Antony Gormley's Another Place, featuring 100 of his signature cast-iron figures, each staring wistfully out to sea.

Spread out along around two miles of foreshore, with others further out to sea, the 650-kilogram figures search the horizon as if anticipating something, creating an atmospheric scene.

Website: www.sefton.gov.uk/default.aspx?page=6216
Address: Access at Hall Road West; Blundellsands Road West
Nearest station: Hall Road; Blundellsands

Step into the Rock Houses at Kinver Edge

Home to England's last troglodyte community until the 1950s, the houses at Kinver Edge in Shropshire (*above*) are hewn out of a rich ridge of rosy sandstone, found beneath an ancient Iron Age fort.

Known as the Holy Austin Rock Houses after a local hermitage, the houses are now owned by the National Trust, and have been restored to look as they would have during the Victorian era, allowing visitors to imagine life as a cave dweller. On cold October days, a warming fire often blazes in the range, keeping damp at bay, whilst on the top level a tea shop is open to visitors.

Website: www.nationaltrust.org.uk/kinver-edge/
Address: Holy Austin Rock Houses, Kinver, near Stourbridge, DY7 6DL
Nearest station: Stourbridge Town

Drink in a Mancunian Public Toilet

One of Manchester's most distinctive bars, the Temple, is a tiny place, built inside a former public toilet on Great Bridgewater Street.

Famous for its Manchester-centric jukebox, its questionable unisex toilet-within-a-toilet, and its capacity of around thirty thirsty Mancunians, the Temple is a favourite with local students seeking a different drinking experience.

Website: www.manchestersfinest.com/drinking-in-manchester/
Address: 100 Great Bridgewater St, Manchester, M1 5JW
Nearest station: Manchester Oxford Road

Celebrate Punkie Night

Punkie Night is a custom observed in the Somerset village of Hinton St George on the last Thursday in October. The event is thought to have links to the ancient fire rites of Celtic Samhain, or to a candle-lit search for inebriated husbands returning from nearby Chiselborough Fair.

The night traditionally sees children touring the village to beg for candles, which they place in scooped-out mangel-wurzels to create lanterns called 'punkies'. These are carved to represent trees, houses or faces and carried through the streets while the 'Punkie Song' is sung.

Website: www.information-britain.co.uk/customdetail.php?id=64
Address: Hinton St George, Somerset
Nearest station: Crewkerne

Search for the Pendle Witches

Even as late as the seventeenth century, the area around Pendle Hill in Lancashire was a wild and untamed part of the country. It is perhaps unsurprising, then, that such a place found itself at the centre of one of the most famous allegations of witchcraft in Protestant England, culminating in the trial and execution of seven women and two men known as the Pendle Witches.

The area remains bleak and eerie even today. On All Hallows' Eve, people climb up Pendle Hill to take part in a hilltop gathering, remembering the impoverished Demdike and Chattox families. Both clans were headed up by haggard widows who damned themselves in the trials by making allegations against each other.

Website: www.visitlancashire.com/explore/pendle-hill
Address: Pendle's Gateway Visitor Centre,
Boundary Mill, Colne, BB8 9NW
Nearest station: Colne

November

As November begins, autumn has its last hurrah, before retreating to make way for the colder months. The days around Guy Fawkes Night on the 5th see communities gathering in fields, public parks and on greens for bonfires and fireworks, which are at their most impressive in Sussex at Battle, Newick and Lewes, Brockham in Surrey, and in Devon at Ottery St Mary, known for its flaming tar barrels.

At this time of year, just a few weekend trippers still make the most of the countryside, enjoying atmospheric autumnal walks, quiet weekends in country hotels and stunning sunsets. As the nights draw in, England's cosy pubs see fires relit, and the bounty of recent harvests is still on show in larders and farmers' markets. Seaside towns are meanwhile busy with autumn arts and music.

Gaze into the Hole of Horcum

The vast Hole of Horcum, 400 feet deep and three-quarters of a mile wide, dominates the valley of the Levisham Beck in the North York Moors. Local mythology links the Hole to Wade, a Saxon warrior chief who is often depicted as a giant thanks to the exaggeration of later storytellers.

Legend has it that Wade grabbed a handful of earth to fling at his wife, and the resulting cavity became the Hole. He missed his wife, however, and a nearby hill is said to be the result. Whatever the history, the Hole is very impressive and makes a good spot for a walk for those with strong legs.

Website: www.holeofhorcum.co.uk
Address: Short walk from Levisham Village
Nearest station: Malton

See the Somerset Carnivals

November is carnival season in Somerset, with the Somerset County Guy Fawkes Carnival Association making a circuit of the county, as it has been doing since the seventeenth century, to commemorate the Gunpowder Plot.

As the nights begin to draw in, up to sixty brightly lit carnival carts travel around the county, lighting up the towns of Bridgwater, North Petherton, Burnham-on-Sea, Shepton Mallet, Wells, Glastonbury and Weston-super-Mare.

Website: www.somersetcountycarnivals.co.uk
Address: Locations across the county of Somerset
Nearest station: Check online for nearest station to each location

Climb the Cabot Tower

The city of Bristol has always been proud of its adopted son, John Cabot, or Giovanni Caboto, an Italian sailor who set out from the port in 1497 to become the first European to reach mainland North America. At the end of the nineteenth century, a tower was erected on top of Bristol's Brandon Hill to celebrate him.

The tower is still open and free to visit, and while its staircase is quite tight, the views from the top are exceptional, as Brandon Hill provides an excellent vantage point for surveying the city.

Website: http://visitbristol.co.uk/things-to-do/cabot-tower-p24401
Address: Brandon Hill, Great George St, Bristol BS1 5RR
Nearest station: Bristol

Walk the Sandstone Trail

Stretching for thirty-four miles across rural Cheshire, the Sandstone Trail follows a ridge of sandstone hills from Frodsham, on the banks of the River Mersey, to Whitchurch, just over the border, in Shropshire.

Along the route, the trail takes in Bronze Age and Iron Age hill forts, Roman roads, medieval churches and castles, and some spectacular views towards Chester and Liverpool. Though it takes two or three days to walk the whole trail, there are plenty of circular day-long walks along the route.

Website: www.sandstonetrail.com
Address: From Frodsham to Whitchurch
Nearest station: Various inc. Frodsham, Delamere and Whitchurch

GO SEAL-SPOTTING
ON BLAKENEY POINT

The North Norfolk coast is home to one of Britain's largest colonies of grey seals, and the breeding season at Blakeney Point Nature Reserve is in full swing by November. Boat trips from Morston and walks along the three-mile sand-and-shingle spit offer the chance to catch a glimpse of the young seals.

Grey seals begin to arrive in September, but the first pups are not usually born until November. As the young pups are restricted to staying on the beach for their first few weeks, this period offers the best chance for discrete seal-watching (though care should always be taken to keep a sensible distance from both adult and young seals).

Website: www.nationaltrust.org.uk/blakeney/
Address: Morston Quay, Morston, NR25 7BH
Nearest station: Sheringham

Celebrate with the Lewes Bonfire Societies

England's most impressive celebrations of Guy Fawkes Night are at Lewes, in Sussex, whose five bonfire societies – Cliffe, Borough, Commercial Square, South Street and Waterloo – compete to build the most impressive inferno, joining together only for the typically anarchic Grand Union Parade, before returning to their own areas for separate huge bonfires.

Though the authorities try to keep the event under control, the evening is marked with a rebellious and riotous air, reminiscent of pre-Victorian times when bonfire celebrations were more spontaneous and had a habit of getting wildly out of control. At the modern celebrations, flaming torches and crosses, ear-bursting firecrackers and burning tar barrels are a key part of the spectacle, drawing thousands of visitors.

Website: www.lewesbonfirecouncil.org.uk
Address: Seven locations across Lewes
Nearest station: Lewes

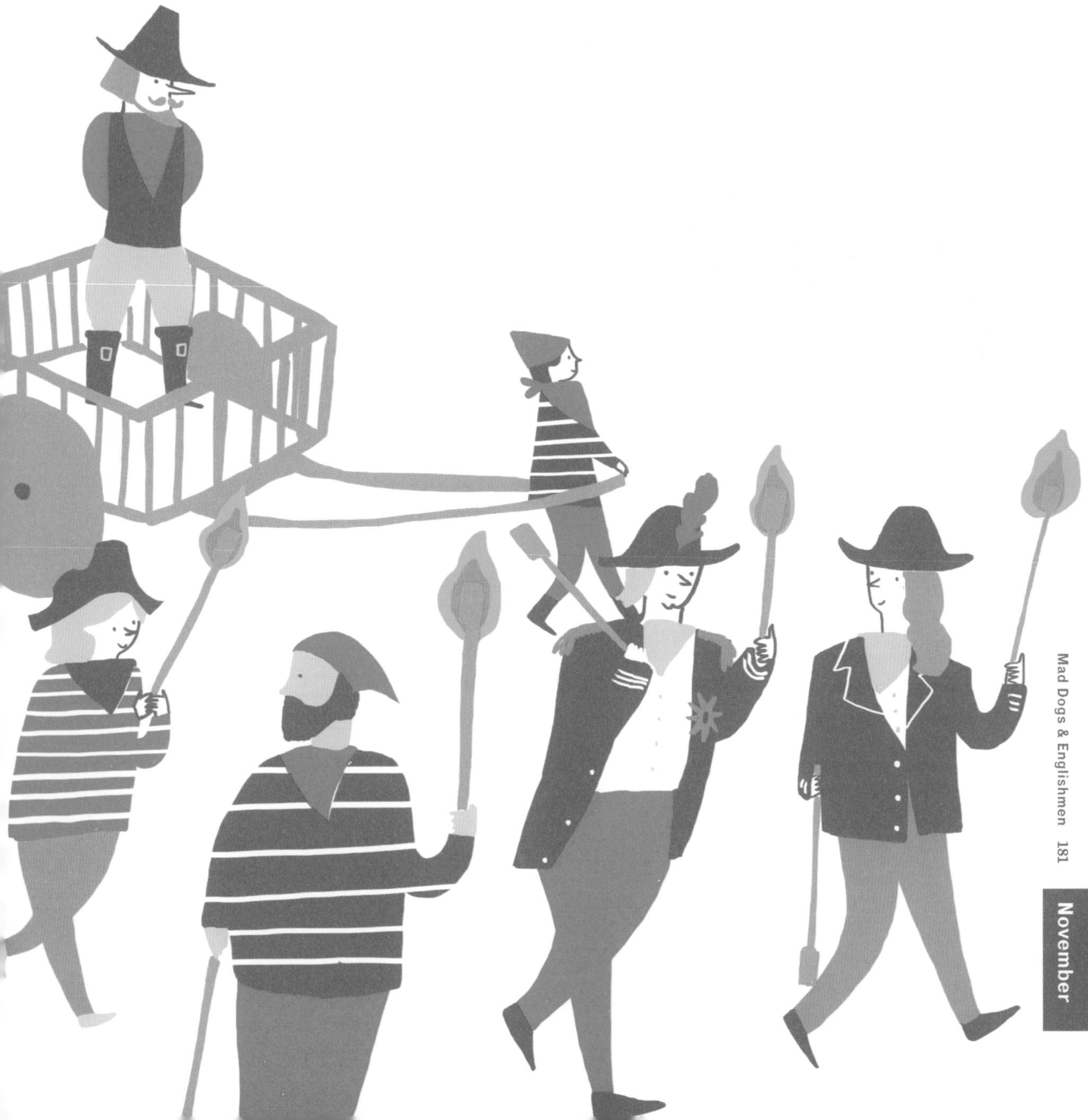

Stand Beside the Brockham Bonfire

Following weeks of bonfire-building, the usually sleepy Surrey village of Brockham comes alive on the Saturday closest to 5 November, as it competes to hold one of the biggest bonfires and firework displays in the country, in a tradition that dates back until at least the 1880s.

The community comes together for an evening of festivities, with (*above*) a procession around neighbouring hamlets by flaming torchlight before the torch-bearers arrive en masse at the village green for the lighting of the bonfire and a spectacular firework display.

Website: www.brockhambonfire.com
Address: Village Green, Brockham, Mole Valley, Surrey
Nearest station: Betchworth, Dorking Deepdene

Visit the Jerwood Gallery at Hastings Stade

Built among the fishermen's huts of Hastings Old Town, the Jerwood Gallery is a relatively new addition to the area, displaying the Jerwood Foundation's collection of modern British art, with a distinctly nautical and Sussex leaning.

Opened in 2012, as part of a massive regeneration project in Hastings, and coexisting with the industrial workings of the local fishing industry, it feels like a fitting addition to the town, with views straight out into the English Channel.

Website: www.jerwoodgallery.org
Address: Rock-a-Nore Road, Hastings, East Sussex TN34 3DW
Nearest station: Hastings

See Malvern's Morgan Museum

The Morgan Motor Company has been making cars in the Worcestershire spa town of Malvern for over 100 years, and continues to do so in the face of the decline of many other British car manufacturers.

The company also has a visitors' centre and museum at its factory in Malvern's Pickersleigh Road, with guided tours of the factory available and interesting exhibitions five days a week, as well as a fine display of Morgan cars.

Website: www.morgan-motor.co.uk /mmc/factoryvisits.html
Address: Pickersleigh Roadɑ, Malvern Link, Malvern, WR14 2LL
Nearest station: Malvern Link

Spend a Night at the Jamaica Inn

Immortalised in Daphne du Maurier's novel of the same name, the Jamaica Inn was built in 1750 as a coaching inn on the vital route from Cornwall to London. Said to have been a haunt for ship-wreckers and other unsavoury types, the inn has its own smugglers museum, which it claims is home to the finest collection of smuggling artefacts in England.

Given the rich history and remote location, it is perhaps unsurprising that previous landlords have reported hearing ghostly footsteps. Legend tells of a stranger murdered immediately after leaving the pub, giving the inn a fearsome reputation among ghost-hunters, many of whom come to seek out apparitions.

Website: www.jamaicainn.co.uk
Address: Jamaica Inn, Bolventor, Launceston, Cornwall, PL15 7TS
Nearest station: Bodmin Parkway

Visit the Home of the Brontë Sisters

The village of Haworth – in which the Brontë sisters found inspiration for their celebrated works – is at its most broodingly melancholic on dark November days. The Brontë Parsonage Museum, once the home of sisters Charlotte, Emily and Anne Brontë, and the place where some of their most famous books were written – including *Jane Eyre*, *Wuthering Heights* and *The Tenant of Wildfell Hall* – is open all year round.

The parsonage stands on the Brontë Way, a footpath stretching across more than forty miles of Yorkshire and Lancashire countryside. The route takes in many key sights from Brontë books, including Wycoller Hall, the inspiration for Ferndean Manor in *Jane Eyre*, and the moors to Top Withins, immortalised on the moors of *Wuthering Heights*.

Website: www.bronte.org.uk
Address: Brontë Parsonage Museum, Church Street, Haworth, West Yorkshire, BD22 8DR
Nearest station: Keighley; Leeds

SEARCH FOR THE WORLD'S BIGGEST LIAR

Nineteenth-century Cumbrian landlord Will Ritson, who lived at the head of the Wasdale Valley in the Lake District, was known for his unbelievable folk tales and his ability to spin a good yarn.

Ritson's memory is kept alive in the form of the World's Biggest Liar Competition, held each November at the Bridge Inn at Santon Bridge, Wasdale, with competitors fighting it out to be crowned 'Biggest Liar in the World', an accolade awarded to the person deemed most worthy of following in the footsteps of 'Auld Will'.

Website: http://santonbridgeinn.com/liar/
Address: Bridge Inn, Santon Bridge, Holmrook, Cumbria CA19 1UX
Nearest station: Drigg

Seek Inspiration at the Turner Contemporary

Once a proud Victorian seaside resort, in many ways the town of Margate in Kent has seen better days. But in 2011, it saw a renaissance, with the opening of the Turner Contemporary gallery on its waterfront. It adopted the name of celebrated landscape painter J M W Turner, who was schooled in the town and maintained an association with it until his death in 1851.

Designed by David Chipperfield Architects, the gallery has large windows offering impressive views of the sea and skies off the North Kent coast. It is situated on the site of the guesthouse owned by Mrs Booth, where Turner stayed during trips to Margate, and where he drew inspiration from the light, once remarking to John Ruskin that, 'The skies over Thanet are the loveliest in all Europe.'

Website: www.turnercontemporary.org
Address: The Rendezvous, Margate, Kent CT9 1HG
Nearest station: Margate

Walk the Coleridge Way

In 1797, poet Samuel Taylor Coleridge moved to Nether Stowey in Somerset, where he remained for three fruitful years. A thirty-six-mile walk, beginning at the cottage in Nether Stowey that is now a museum of his life, takes walkers to Porlock. Coleridge would often take this route for inspiration, and presumably it is the same walk taken by the 'Person from Porlock' who interrupted Coleridge's writing of *Kubla Khan*, a poem about the Mongol emperor.

For a shorter walk, an interesting section passes Alfoxton House at Holford, home to William Wordsworth during the same period, and heads across the Quantocks to Watchet. Wordsworth's memoirs recall this November walk with Coleridge, noting that 'in the course of this walk was planned the poem of *The Rime of the Ancient Mariner*, founded on a dream'.

Website: www.coleridgeway.co.uk
Address: The Quantock Hills, the Brendon Hills and Exmoor
Nearest station: Bridgwater; Taunton

See the Imperial War Museum North

Situated on the banks of the Manchester Ship Canal in Salford, the Imperial War Museum North opened in 2002 to complement the museum's other operations in Duxford and London.

The museum's distinctive aluminium-clad building was designed by architect Daniel Libeskind, and has attracted more than 2 million visitors in the decade since its opening. Unlike its southern sister, the museum offers the added benefit of being situated in a purpose-built structure in which space is optimised.

Website: www.iwm.org.uk/visits/iwm-north
Address: The Quays, Trafford Wharf Road, Manchester M17 1TZ
Nearest station: Manchester Piccadilly

Learn about Grimsby's Fishing Heritage

Grimsby's Fishing Heritage Centre opened at Alexandra Dock in 1991, its aim to tell the story of the town's fishing heritage, with a particular focus on what life was like for trawlermen and their families in the 1950s.

The museum offers the chance to climb aboard the *Ross Tiger*, a 1950s trawler that was acquired by the town in 1992 for just one pound and is now moored beside the museum.

Website: www.nelincs.gov.uk/resident/museums-and-heritage
Address: Alexandra Dock, Grimsby, N E Lincolnshire, DN31 1UZ
Nearest station: Grimsby Docks

Spend an Hour at the Coalface

A trip to the National Coal Mining Museum in Wakefield offers the chance to descend into a former coal mine and take a tour with former miners, getting an insight into life at the coalface.

The museum was opened in 1988 on the site of the eighteenth-century Caphouse Colliery – a mine that closed in 1985 – and today offers an insight into what life was like for miners and their families when the industry was at its height.

Website: www.ncm.org.uk
Address: Caphouse Colliery New Rd, Overton, West Yorkshire WF4 4RH
Nearest station: Wakefield Westgate

Walk Saltfleetby and Theddlethorpe Dunes

The dunes at Saltfleet, on the Lincolnshire coast, only began to form in the thirteenth century, and continue to move slowly as they are buffeted by wind and tide.

As winter approaches, the area is a good place to spot thousands of wildfowl, with Brent geese, shelduck and feeding waders flocking to this stretch of coast. Occasional remnants of wrecked military tanks litter the shore, as it was once used for target practice when the marshes were a bombing range.

Website: www.theddlethorpe.org.uk/nature.htm
Address: Access at Churchill Lane, Brickyard Lane and Crook Bank
Nearest station: Cleethorpes

REMEMBER THE FALLEN AT THE NATIONAL MEMORIAL ARBORETUM

As the country holds memorial services around 11 November each year, the Armed Forces Memorial at the National Memorial Arboretum in Alrewas, Staffordshire, marks the occasion in a truly poignant way. The memorial is aligned so that, at the eleventh hour of the eleventh day of the eleventh month, the Sun's rays stream through its door, illuminating a wreath in the centre.

The Armed Forces Memorial honours those members of the Armed Forces who have lost their lives in service since the end of the Second World War, and is one of scores of memorials at the Arboretum, which boasts more than 50,000 trees.

Website: www.thenma.org.uk/
Address: Croxall Rd, Alrewas, Staffordshire DE13 7AR
Nearest station: Lichfield Trent Valley

Buy a Paperback at Barter Books

A huge second-hand bookshop located in the Victorian station building in Alnwick, Northumberland, Barter Books boasts scores of categorised bookshelves dotted with comfortable reading areas and a model train chuffing its way around the tops of the shelves.

The architecture of the old station is preserved within the shop to create a grand setting. And if visitors can manage to work their way past many thousands of books, a cosy welcome awaits in the Station Buffet, where hot and cold drinks and hearty cakes and meals are served beside roaring coal fires.

Website: www.barterbooks.co.uk
Address: Alnwick Station, Wagon Way Rd, Alnwick, NE66 2NP
Nearest station: Alnmouth

Explore the Beatles' Liverpool

In early November 1961, the Beatles took to the stage at the Cavern Club in Liverpool to begin a series of local gigs that continued until the end of the year. It was during this tour that the Beatles first started to create a buzz in the city, and that Brian Epstein – their celebrated manager – first saw them play.

Today, the Beatles are synonymous with Liverpool, with Lennon and McCartney's childhood homes in the care of the National Trust and a re-creation of the Cavern Club open to the public. Thirsty fans also head to the Grapes in Matthew Street – where the Beatles were known to drink between their gigs – and undertake pilgrimages to Penny Lane and Strawberry Fields.

Website: www.cavernclub.org
Address: Cavern City Tours, Century Buildings, 31 North John Street, Liverpool L2 6RG
Nearest station: Liverpool

Watch the Lord Mayor's Show

The City of London's Lord Mayor's Show has been an annual tradition since around 1215, when King John granted a charter to allow the citizens of London to elect a mayor. Around 800 years later, having survived despite two plagues, two world wars and the Great Fire, the show is still held on the second Saturday in November to welcome the appointment of the new Lord Mayor.

Crowds line the streets to watch a procession over three miles, involving more than 6,000 participants, which leads the new Lord Mayor to the Royal Courts of Justice. There he takes an oath of allegiance. The day usually ends with a fireworks display over the Thames between Blackfriars Bridge and Waterloo Bridge.

Website: www.lordmayorsshow.org
Address: From Mansion House to the Royal Courts of Justice in Aldwych
Nearest station: London Euston

WALK IN ENGLAND'S ONLY DESERT

A huge expanse of shingle on the Kentish coast, Dungeness, is home to ramshackle fishing huts, a lighthouse, two pubs and a nuclear power station. The peninsula is otherwise largely devoid of features or vegetation and is officially classified as the only desert in the British Isles.

The area has long attracted artists, drawn there by the spectacular contrasts of shingle, sea and sky, and the sense of remoteness offered by views out to sea. The unusual landscapes make the area a popular spot for birds, and in November, marsh harriers are regularly spotted, as are greenfinches, siskins and chaffinches, arriving for the winter months.

Website: www.rspb.org.uk/reserves/guide/d/dungeness/about.aspx
Address: RSPB Dungeness Nature Reserve, Boulderwell Farm, Dungeness Road, Lydd, Kent, TN29 9PN
Nearest station: Rye; Ashford; Folkestone

Gaze Out from South Foreland Lighthouse

In late November 1703, Southern England was hit by a storm greater than any other. Scores of ships were wrecked on Goodwin Sands in the English Channel, as immortalised in Daniel Defoe's *The Storm*. In 1730, a lighthouse was established at South Foreland, on the white cliffs near Dover, to protect ships from the dangerous sands.

The current building – now open to the public – is a successor to the original, and was the first lighthouse to use an electric light. It was also the scene of many of Guglielmo Marconi's experiments with radio waves, receiving both the first ship-to-shore message, from the East Goodwin lightship, and the first international radio transmission, sent from Wimereux on the French coast in 1899.

Website: www.nationaltrust.org.uk/south-foreland-lighthouse
Address: The Front, Dover, CT15 6HP
Nearest station: Dover

Go to the Top of Blackpool Tower

First opened to the public in 1894, Blackpool Tower is a Grade I-listed building rising more than 500 feet above the seafront, and designed to mirror the Eiffel Tower in Paris.

Despite the rather odd cinema experience that visitors must endure before being allowed to ride the lift to the top, the views are worth the effort, giving an interesting perspective on the scale of the seaside economy in Blackpool, a chance to see the iconic piers and fine views out to sea.

Website: www.theblackpooltower.com
Address: The Blackpool Tower The Promenade Blackpool FY1 4BJ
Nearest station: Blackpool North

Eat Dinner on Manchester's Curry Mile

A short bus ride from central Manchester, the Curry Mile runs along Wilmslow Road through the centre of Rusholme. The area is a focus of the city's Asian communities, and scores of restaurants are found along the strip, with a number specialising in South Asian cuisine.

In recent years, the growth of the local Middle Eastern and Afghan communities has led to diversification in the restaurants here, and also a proliferation of shisha bars.

Website: www.manchesterrestaurants.com/rusholme.htm
Address: Wilmslow Road, Rusholme, Greater Manchester
Nearest station: Manchester Piccadilly

Read at Chetham's Library

First founded by cloth merchant Humphrey Chetham, in 1653, Chetham's Library in Manchester is the oldest surviving public library in Britain. Its medieval buildings were the first meeting place of Karl Marx and Friedrich Engels, and the desk at which they worked can still be seen today.

Now operated as a charity, the library holds more than 100,000 books and is open for the public to tour on weekdays. It is available to readers free of charge with a prior appointment, as stipulated in Chetham's will.

Website: www.chethams.org.uk
Address: Chetham's Library, Long Millgate, M3 1SB
Nearest station: Manchester Victoria

Sit by the Fire at the Lion Inn, Blakey Ridge

A sixteenth-century freehouse on a remote ridge in the North York Moors, the Lion Inn at Blakey Ridge stands at an elevation of 1,325 feet, on the long moorland road between Hutton-Le-Hole and Castleton.

Though the inn is occasionally cut off by snow for more than a week at a time during the winter months, when it is open it offers a warm fireside welcome with ale and good food in an inspiring setting. Describing the Lion Inn as the best pub for miles around probably doesn't do it justice.

Website: www.lionblakey.co.uk
Address: Lion Inn, Blakey Ridge, North Yorks. YO62 7LQ
Nearest station: Castleton Moor; Castleton

Stand Beneath High Force

When bolstered by autumn rains, High Force, England's biggest waterfall in the North Pennines at Teesdale, is an impressive sight as the River Tees drops more than seventy feet into a dark pool below.

The height of the waterfall is a result of local geology, with the river dropping over the Whin Sill, a hard layer of igneous dolerite, which takes longer than many other rocks to be eroded by water.

Website: www.rabycastle.com/High_Force_Waterfall
Address: High Force Waterfall Forest-in-Teesdale,
Co. Durham DL12 0XH
Nearest station: Darlington

SEE ROALD DAHL'S WRITING HUT

Every writer needs a place to write, and for Roald Dahl, the much-loved children's author, this place was a hut at the bottom of his garden. The hut was built in the 1950s and was used by Dahl for the rest of his life as a place to escape and to formulate his books.

In 2012, the hut was transported from Dahl's garden at Gipsy House, Great Missenden, to the nearby Roald Dahl Museum, where it is now on display. The hut has been kept just as it was when Dahl died in 1990, complete with his famous wing-backed writing chair, which had been adapted to ease the back pain he suffered as the result of a wartime injury.

Website: www.roalddahlmuseum.org
Address: 81-83 High Street, Great Missenden, Bucks., HP16 0AL
Nearest station: Great Missenden

Notes

....

....

....

....

....

....

....

December

Winter has firmly arrived, and as the last of the autumn leaves fall off the trees, the remaining evergreen foliage is brought inside in the form of Christmas trees and holly, to keep the memory of summer greens alive. As midwinter approaches, cold weather and short days spark feasting and seasonal celebrations: a combination of Christian, Victorian, pagan and modern rituals play out in towns and villages, with midwinter church services, advent fairs, mummers plays and other traditions.

Before the year ends, communities come together with a New Year's Eve party, marked most dramatically by the flaming tar barrels that stalk the streets of Allendale in Northumberland, and by fireworks and revelry in every town, village and hamlet.

Visit the Scott Polar Research Institute

Founded in 1920, as a memorial to the members of Scott's Antarctic expedition who perished on their return from the South Pole in 1912, the Scott Polar Research Institute in Cambridge investigates issues relevant to both poles.

The institute's museum uses a range of art and artefacts to tell the story of polar exploration, and the history and science of the polar regions. Special events mark Antarctica Day, 1 December, in recognition of the 1959 Antarctic Treaty.

Website: www.spri.cam.ac.uk/
Address: Lensfield Road, Cambridge CB2 1EP
Nearest station: Cambridge

Sing Yorkshire Village Carols in Dungworth

Once popular across the country, village carols have been kept alive in a handful of communities around England. Possibly sung for even longer than the Christmas carols that mark the modern festive season, they are distinctive and regional and as likely to be sung in a pub as in a church.

The village of Dungworth, on the outskirts of Sheffield, is the keeper of the Yorkshire tradition, with carols sung with gusto every Sunday lunchtime at the Royal Hotel, from the Sunday after Armistice Day to Boxing Day.

Website: www.royalhotel-dungworth.co.uk
Address: Main Road, Dungworth, Sheffield S6 1EF
Nearest station: Sheffield or Meadowhall Interchange

Wander the Rows of Chester

A distinctive aspect of Chester's city centre, the Chester Rows are half-timbered galleries accessed via steps, forming a second row of shops above those at street level. A feature of the streets radiating from Chester Cross, the Rows are found in Watergate, Eastgate and Northgate Streets and also in Upper Bridge Street.

Though the origins of the Rows are subject to debate, it is thought that they date from at least the thirteenth century, when they were possibly built by medieval traders on top of crumbling Roman debris, or designed to prevent a repeat of a fire that all but destroyed the city in 1278.

Website: www.visitchester.com/things-to-do/chester-rows-p22731
Address: Bridge St, Watergate St, Eastgate Street in Chester
Nearest station: Chester

See Dunster by Candlelight

Each year, on the first Friday and Saturday in December, to mark the start of the festive season, the medieval Somerset village of Dunster rejects the modern world and returns to using candles to light its streets.

The event starts with a lantern-lighting procession and includes carol singers, hand-bell ringers, stalls and street entertainers, and is paid for by the traders of the village as a way of encouraging people to consider Dunster for their Christmas shopping.

Website: www.dunsterbycandlelight.co.uk
Address: Dunster Steep, Dunster, Somerset
Nearest station: Taunton

Drink at 'England's Oldest Inn'

One of a number of pubs claiming to be England's oldest, the Bingley Arms in the Yorkshire village of Bardsley can trace its history back at least as far as AD 953, when a man called Samson Ellis is known to have been brewing in part of the building that is still used today. The owners believe the pub probably dates from more than fifty years before that, around AD 905.

Previously known as the Priest's Inn, the pub was a place of refuge for members of the clergy during times of Catholic persecution, and its chimney contains two priest holes, dating back to 1539, in which priests hid from the authorities.

Website: www.bingleyarms.co.uk
Address: The Bingley Arms Church Lane, Bardsey, Leeds, LS17 9DR
Nearest station: Leeds

Walk in Hadleigh Country Park

The tidal creeks between Benfleet and Leigh-on-Sea are particularly beautiful, and are overlooked by Hadleigh Castle, an impressive thirteenth-century construction refortified during the Hundred Years' War. This was the stomping ground of James Murrell, the last witch doctor in England, who is buried at Hadleigh Church and who correctly foretold the date of his death in December 1860.

Between the castle and the creekside, Hadleigh Country Park offers more than 350 acres of parkland, with a mix of woodland, grassland and marsh. A bridge just outside the park enables walkers to cross to the Essex Wildlife Trust's nature reserve at Two Tree Island.

Website: www.hadleighcountrypark.co.uk
Address: Chapel Lane, Benfleet SS7 2PP
Nearest station: Benfleet

Join the Broughton Tin Can Band

The Devil is beaten out of the Northamptonshire village of Broughton just before midnight on the first Sunday after 12 December by a rowdy bunch of locals who make up the Broughton Tin Can Band.

The custom sees the banging of tin cans, pans, kettles and anything that will make a noise, and is thought to be linked to Old St Andrew's Day. Once on the verge of dying out, the tradition was given a new lease of life in 1929 when the local council decided to ban it, prompting a strong turnout from locals and a public outcry when they were arrested.

Website: www.calendarcustoms.com/articles/broughton-tin-can-band
Address: Broughton, Northamptonshire near St Andrew's Church
Nearest station: Kettering

EXPERIENCE AN AMERICAN CHRISTMAS

The only museum of Americana outside the United States, the American Museum in Britain was opened in July 1961 at Claverton Manor, near Bath.

Founded by American collector Dallas Pratt and British antiques dealer John Judkyn, the museum is home to displays on all aspects of American heritage. In the run-up to Christmas each year, the rooms of the museum are rearranged for a seasonal display featuring unique handmade decorations.

Website: www.americanmuseum.org
Address: The American Museum in Britain, Claverton Manor, Bath BA2 7BD
Nearest station: Bath Spa

GO INCOGNITO AT THE OLD SWAN HOTEL

On the evening of Friday 3 December 1926, the writer Agatha Christie kissed her daughter goodnight at their home, Styles in Berkshire, and set off into the night. Her car was later found abandoned at Newlands Corner near Guildford, with its famous driver nowhere to be seen.

For eleven days, the nation was gripped with the search for Christie, with great speculation about her whereabouts and the reasons for her disappearance. Eventually, she was located at the Swan Hydropathic Hotel – now The Old Swan Hotel in Harrogate – having checked in alone under an assumed name. Christie never explained her disappearance, and perhaps the secret is still to be found at the grand hotel.

Website: www.classiclodges.co.uk/The_Old_Swan_Hotel_Harrogate
Address: The Old Swan Swan Road, Harrogate, North Yorks., HG1 2SR
Nearest station: Harrogate

Watch the Crowning of the Hereford Boy Bishop

As part of a medieval custom, a Boy Bishop is appointed at Hereford each year on the Sunday closest to 6 December, the Feast of Saint Nicholas, replacing the Bishop on his throne, leading prayer and preaching a sermon he has written himself.

The reign of the Boy Bishop lasts for three weeks, with the traditional role-reversal part of Hereford Cathedral's Christmas season. The tradition was once prevalent around the country, with a choirboy taking on the ceremonial role.

Website: www.herefordcathedral.org
Address: 5 College Cloisters, Cathedral Close, Hereford, HR1 2NG
Nearest station: Hereford

See the Winster Guisers

For centuries, mummers plays have offered live interpretations of folk tales, originally toured around local houses and pubs by performers wanting to raise a few pennies.

In and around the village of Winster in Derbyshire, December is mumming season. There are numerous opportunities to see the Winster Guisers perform their play at various pubs and public places, with characters and costumes inspired by Victorian accounts of a play in the village.

Website: www.peakdistrictonline.co.uk
Address: Winster Village and other White Peak Derbyshire venues
Nearest station: Matlock

Stock up on Wines at Malpas Stallard

An institution in Worcester, wine merchant Malpas Stallard combines two historic wine-sellers, Joseph Malpas and Company (established in 1807) and Josiah Stallard and Sons (trading since 1808 by a family known to have been selling wine since the reign of Henry VII).

In 1969, the two companies combined, moving to the historic cellars of Josiah Stallard in Fish Street, where they still trade today, offering centuries of wine expertise.

Website: www.malpasstallard.co.uk
Address: The Cellars, Fish Street, Worcester, WR1 2HN
Nearest station: Worcester

Watch the Sunset at Whitstable

One of the few places on the East Coast where the sun sets over the sea, Whitstable in Kent offers some dramatic sunsets when the conditions are right, and the show in December can be particularly special.

The welcoming warmth of the Old Neptune pub on the West Beach offers a comfortable setting for watching the light of the sun slowly disappear. Visitors will often be treated to a beautiful display of reds, oranges and yellows as night begins.

Website: www.neppy.co.uk
Address: Marine Terrace, Whitstable, CT5 1EJ
Nearest station: Whitstable

Drive on Britain's
First Motorway

When it was opened by Prime Minister Harold Macmillan on 5 December 1958, the Preston By-pass was Britain's first stretch of motorway. Now incorporated into the M6 between Junctions 29 and 32, the original by-pass had just two lanes in each direction, separated by a hedge.

The Preston By-pass pilot scheme literally paved the way for the transport network that today stretches to all corners of the country, but at the time it covered just over eight miles from Bamber Bridge to Broughton, where it ended at a roundabout on the A6 to the north of Preston.

Website: www.madeinpreston.co.uk/Road/M6.html
Address: Runs from Bamber Bridge to Broughton
Nearest station: Preston (Lancs.)

Hunt for Fossils on
the Jurassic Coast

While a pair of gloves is essential in cold weather, the first calm low tide after a period of wild winter weather is the perfect time to search for fossils along Dorset's Jurassic coast. The area between Lyme Regis and Charmouth offers some of the best chances in England of finding ammonite, reptile, fish and belemnite fossils among the rocks.

Extreme care should be taken to avoid falling rocks and do take notice of warning signs along the coast. More information is available from the Charmouth Heritage Coast Centre, which also organises fossil-hunting walks.

Website: www.charmouth.org/chcc/
Address: Lower Sea Lane, Charmouth, Dorset, DT6 6LL
Nearest station: Axminster

Go Christmas Shopping
in York

The medieval streets of York are a fine place to stock up on Christmas gifts, lit with twinkling lights in the shadow of York Minster, the stunning cathedral that hosts evening carol services.

Dotted with characterful independent shops – as well as a tolerable number of larger chains – the city holds Christmas markets and is known for its tea rooms and pubs, offering a warming escape if a wintry chill hits.

Website: www.historyofyork.org.uk/themes/medieval/the-shambles
Address: The Shambles, York
Nearest station: York

Go Curling at Fenton's Rink

England's only dedicated curling rink is found at Dundale Farm near Tunbridge Wells in Kent. It was opened in November 2004, in response to Great Britain's success in curling at the 2002 Winter Olympics in Salt Lake City.

Curling began on the frozen ponds of Scotland, and it is no coincidence that Ernest Fenton, the creator of Fenton's Rink, is a Scot, who built the rink in order to bring the sport back to the UK.

Website: www.fentonsrink.co.uk
Address: Fenton's Rink, Dundale Farm, Tunbridge Wells TN3 9AQ
Nearest station: Tunbridge Wells

Celebrate Montol in Penzance

A revival of an ancient Cornish midwinter festival, Montol is celebrated in and around Penzance in the days leading up to Montol Eve, which coincides with the winter solstice.

The festival features a range of events, including lantern processions, an appearance from the Montol Lord of Misrule, music from the Turkey Rhubarb Guise Band and a ceremony to mark the chalking and burning of the Mock, the Cornish Yule log.

Website: www.montol.co.uk
Address: Penzance, Cornwall
Nearest station: Penzance

Observe the Solstice at Stonehenge

While Stonehenge (*above*) is more commonly associated with the summer solstice, a smaller but more dedicated group of sun-worshippers gather at the site in December to mark the winter solstice, with English Heritage often allowing access into the circle of stones, an opportunity not usually available to visitors.

Alongside the inevitable neo-druids and pagans, many people travel from the surrounding area and further afield to observe the sunrise on the shortest day of the year, and to begin the uphill journey back towards summer.

Website: www.stonehenge.co.uk
Address: Amesbury, Wiltshire, UK
Nearest station: Salisbury

SEE THE MOUSEHOLE CHRISTMAS LIGHTS

In the early 1960s, in an attempt to provide some seasonal cheer to the Cornish fishing village of Mousehole, local artist Joan Gillchrest put up a string of twinkling lights around the quayside. Today, the lights – which display Christmas themes and old village stories and legends – have become an annual tradition in the tiny harbour, and visitors travel from miles around to see them.

The celebrations come to a head on Tom Bawcock's Eve, 23 December, when locals remember sixteenth-century fisherman, Tom Bawcock. When no other boats were able to fish and the residents faced starvation, Tom set out onto a stormy sea and returned with fish for everyone, just in time for Christmas. The festival still sees the making of Stargazy Pie, a pie of baked pilchards, egg and potatoes, with the heads of the pilchards poking out to look up at the stars and prove there are fish inside.

Website: www.mouseholelights.org.uk
Address: Quayside, Mousehole, Cornwall
Nearest station: Penzance

Hear the Devil's Knell

At Dewsbury Minster in South Yorkshire, the final minutes of Christmas Eve are marked by the 'tolling of the Devil's knell', as bell-ringers gather to ring 'Black Tom' – a tenor bell named after local landowner Sir Thomas De Soothill – once for every year since the birth of Christ.

The tolling begins at around 10 p.m., with one stroke every few seconds, and is timed to end at midnight, symbolising the defeat of Satan when Jesus was born, and supposedly keeping the Devil out of Dewsbury for another year.

Website: www.dewsburyminster.org.uk/the-bells/
Address: Dewsbury Minster, Rishworth Road, Dewsbury, WF12 8DD
Nearest station: Dewsbury

Visit the Churchyard that Inspired a Dickensian Tale

St James's church in the Kent village of Cooling is a dramatic place, with sweeping views across the Hoo Peninsula towards the Thames. The church, now in the care of the Churches Conservation Trust, also hides a literary secret: it is the setting for Charles Dickens's opening scene in *Great Expectations*, in which a young Pip meets escaped convict Magwitch for the first time on a bleak Christmas Eve in the churchyard.

In one of his most poignant passages, Dickens records the graves of thirteen children as 'little stone lozenges each about a foot and a half long, which were arranged in a neat row'. These graves are still in place today, marking the resting place of children killed by marsh fever.

Website: www.coolingchurch.org.uk
Address: St James' Church, Cooling, Nr Rochester, Kent ME3 8DG
Nearest station: Higham

Do the Hunstanton Christmas Swim

For more than fifty years, the people of Hunstanton in Norfolk have been celebrating Christmas by charging headlong into the North Sea and swimming in its chilly waters.

Each year, over 100 people show up to brave the waves, with the swim taking place at 11 a.m.. It attracts some swimmers who raise funds for charity, some in fancy dress and others who just enjoy a challenge ahead of a warming Christmas lunch at home.

Website: www.hunstantonroundtable.com/xmas-swim.html
Address: Hunstanton Promenade, Norfolk
Nearest station: Kings Lynn

WATCH THE PAGHAM PRAM RACE

Billing itself as the oldest race of its kind in the world, the Pagham Pram Race is an annual Boxing Day event in this small Sussex Village. The first race took place in 1946, when a group of servicemen, recently demobilised after the Second World War, raced through the streets with a variety of prams in the hope of winning a Christmas fruitcake. The course saw the men run around the village, stopping at each pub they came to, where they would drink a pint of ale before continuing on their way.

Nowadays, up to sixty participants, many of them raising funds for local charities, take part in the three-mile course, which takes them to the Bear Inn, the Lamb Inn and the Kings Beach Hotel, before returning to finish at the Lamb Inn car park.

Website: www.paghampramrace.com
Address: Starting point is Mill Farm, Downlands Close on Pagham Road, Nyetimber, West Sussex
Nearest station: Bognor Regis; Chichester

See the Marshfield Mummers

A traditional mummers play is the highlight of Boxing Day in the town of Marshfield in Gloucestershire, where a local group called the Old Time Paper Boys turns out to perform a play each year.

The Marshfield mummers perform their play several times along the High Street, wearing costumes featuring strips of coloured paper. Christmas hymns precede the performance of the play in the Market Place around 11 a.m, and the performers' approach is announced by a ringing bell.

Website: www.cotswolds.info/strange-things/mummers-plays.shtml
Address: High Street, Marshfield, Gloucestershire
Nearest station: Bath Spa; Oldfield Park

Visit Imber Ghost Village

For most of the year, the village of Imber on the Salisbury Plain is strictly off-limits, cut off by Army training, which has taken place here since the village was evacuated in 1943. The Army does, however, allow access for up to fifty days of the year, often including the period between Christmas and New Year.

At this time of year, the village is particularly eerie, with shells of bomb-damaged houses surrounded by acres of empty Wiltshire countryside, and only the Grade II-listed church of St Giles intact. The church holds occasional services to remember a village that is no more.

Website: www.imberchurch.org.uk
Address: St Giles Church, Imber, Warminster, Wiltshire
Nearest station: Warminster

Seek the Wayfarer's Dole

The Hospital of St Cross and Almshouse of Noble Poverty in Winchester was founded in the 1130s by Henry of Blois, grandson of William the Conqueror, to aid thirteen men unable to work.

Today, alongside continued support for its resident 'brothers', the institution welcomes visitors at certain times to learn its history. It is also known for offering ancient Wayfarer's Dole, and visitors who request it may receive a horn mug of beer and a morsel of bread from the porter's lodge at no charge, according to tradition.

Website: http://stcrosshospital.co.uk
Address: Hospital of St Cross, St Cross Road, Winchester, SO23 9SD
Nearest station: Winchester

Watch a Film at Britain's Oldest Cinema

First opened to the public on 27 December 1909, the Electric Cinema in Birmingham is the oldest working cinema in Britain. At the time, most homes in the city were without electricity, and the films shown were silent, accompanied by piano music.

Rebuilt in 1937, the Electric served variously as a news, pornographic and art-house cinema before closing in 2003. In 2004, following refurbishment, it reopened and is once again attracting film-lovers from Birmingham and beyond.

Website: www.theelectric.co.uk
Address: Electric Cinema, 47–49 Station Street, Birmingham, B5 4DY
Nearest station: Birmingham

Explore the Lewes of Thomas Paine

Thanks to his support of American independence, Thomas Paine was reviled by the English, with effigies of him burned across the nation in December 1792.

Now celebrated for his work as a political activist and writer, Thomas Paine first became involved in politics in Lewes, Sussex. He lived at Bull House on the High Street, debated at the White Hart Hotel and got married at St Michael's Church. A plaque at the White Hart describes the hotel as 'a cradle of American independence'.

Website: www.historyguide.org/intellect/paine.html
Address: Various locations, Lewes, East Sussex
Nearest station: Lewes

Join the Festival of Winter Walks

The annual Festival of Winter Walks runs between Christmas and New Year, organised by the various regional branches of the Ramblers, the national charity that promotes walking and has more than 100,000 members.

Over a week, the Ramblers organise hundreds of walks around the country, taking care to ensure a significant number are under five miles long and suitable for families; and including special themed walks in the hope of enticing people outdoors during the Christmas period.

Website: www.ramblers.org.uk
Address: Throughout England, Scotland and Wales
Nearest station: Various, see site for details

Attend the Allendale Tar Bar'l Festival

Held every New Year's Eve, the Tar Bar'l Festival in Allendale, Northumberland, sees the town ablaze as flaming tar barrels are marched through the streets in an ancient custom. A select team of forty-five fancy-dressed barrel 'guisers' each carry a 15-kilogram flaming-hot barrel of tar through the streets to the town centre, where at midnight, they ignite a ceremonial bonfire.

Website: www.visitnorthumberland.com/allendale
Address: Allendale, Northumberland
Nearest station: Hexham

INDEX